Word in Season
Devotional
First Quarter – Winter

Written by: Earl Cooper, Ph. D
www.DiscipleshipMinistries.ca

ὁ λόγοσ ἐν τῷ λαῷ   ὁ λαόσ ἐν τῷ λόγῳ

Published by:
A Word in Season Ministries
1248 Healey Lake Road
Bracebridge, Ontario, Canada

For additional publications see:
www.AWordInSeasonMinistries.com

A note from Earl:

While pastoring in Bracebridge, Ontario the Lord opened the door for me to write a weekly Bible Devotion newspaper column. This provided a wonderful means of sharing God's word in a broad public format. Over the years of these newspaper column submissions I received many notes of appreciation.

Although I was unable to carry on this column after joining ABWE Canada as a travelling teacher, I added a selection of these devotional submissions to my website to offer a full year of daily devotions for the many who continued to request them. The expressed appreciation of the website devotionals led to publication of these as four Daily Devotion Books – Winter, Spring, Summer, Fall.

It has never been my intention to encourage God's people to substitute written Daily Bible Devotions for daily, personal Bible reading and Bible study. I urge each reader to be encouraged by these devotional thoughts personally, and to use these devotions to minister to others by any means appropriate. However, I also urge each reader to go beyond reading Bible devotions written by myself, or any other, and develop the essential Christian disciplines of systematically reading through the entire Bible regularly, daily studying the Bible inductively, and writing your own Bible Devotion Journals of what God has taught you through study. Although the labour is demanding work, the rewards are 'out of this world.'

Be diligent to present yourself approved to God,
<u>a worker</u> who does not need to be ashamed, rightly
dividing the word of truth.   2 Timothy 2:15
"It is written, 'Man shall not live by bread alone, but by
<u>every word</u> that proceeds from the mouth of God.'"
Matthew. 4:4

Psalm 27:7-14

Hear, O LORD, when I cry with my voice! Have mercy also upon me, and answer me. When You said, "Seek My face," My heart said to You, "Your face, LORD, I will seek." Do not hide Your face from me; Do not turn Your servant away in anger; You have been my help; Do not leave me nor forsake me, O God of my salvation. When my father and my mother forsake me, Then the LORD will take care of me. Teach me Your way, O LORD, And lead me in a smooth path, because of my enemies. Do not deliver me to the will of my adversaries; For false witnesses have risen against me, And such as breathe out violence. I would have lost heart, unless I had believed that I would see the goodness of the LORD In the land of the living. Wait on the LORD; Be of good courage, And He shall strengthen your heart; Wait, I say, on the LORD!

A Friend for All Seasons

For many, looking back on the previous year is a matter of counting blessings and enjoying fond memories. However, there are others who look back on this past year as a single wave of destruction that passed as a blur, leaving only the sense of loss. These are people who understand by personal experience the depth of feeling behind Job's words, "Men groan from out of the city, and the soul of the wounded cries out." (Job 24:12) The word "groan" comes from a term that means pierced or stabbed and here refers to a person who has been wounded of heart, as Job was in the loss of his family and wealth all within a twenty-four hour period. Yet in his cry, his associates responded with calloused hearts and sharp tongues. Those he thought to be friends failed him in his day of need.

Today many hearts have been pierced with personal or economic loss, and like Job, cry out from their hearts only to find rebuke and accusation returned as answer to their hurt. And yet there is reason not to despair, for in the story of Job we are reminded that God never abandons those who put their trust in him: "the LORD blessed the latter end of Job more than at the beginning" (Job 42:12). To all who will trust in God, he proves to be that special friend that sticks closer than a brother (Proverbs 18:24).

For all those hearts that have been pierced this past year and now groan within, there is hope for healing! Jesus, through love that led Him to die for us and power that raised Him from death, secured

4

the restoration of the whole man. He alone can truthfully say "The Spirit of the Lord [is] upon me, because he hath anointed me to preach the gospel to the poor; he hath sent me to heal the broken-hearted, to preach deliverance to the captives, and recovering of sight to the blind, to set at liberty them that are bruised" (Luke 4:18). He, as a true friend that loves at all times, never turns a deaf ear nor a cold shoulder to those who cry in pain for His help. And in turning to Him we are taught to lay our cares and hurts at his feet, because He cares for us (1 Peter 5:7). Perhaps James Small penned this best when he wrote this hymn stanza: "I've found a friend, O such a Friend! He loved me ere I knew Him; He drew me with the cords of love and thus He bound me to Him. And round my heart still closely twine those ties which naught can sever, for I am His and He is mine, forever and forever." This friend that Job and James found (though years and distance apart) wants to be your friend too. Will you make him so?

Personal Notes

Galatians 5:13-25

*For you, brethren, have been called to liberty; only do not use liberty
as an opportunity for the flesh, but through love serve one another.
For all the law is fulfilled in one word, even in this: "You shall love
your neighbour as yourself." But if you bite and devour one another,
beware lest you be consumed by one another! I say then: Walk in the
Spirit, and you shall not fulfill the lust of the flesh. For the flesh lusts
against the Spirit, and the Spirit against the flesh; and these are
contrary to one another, so that you do not do the things that you wish.
But if you are led by the Spirit, you are not under the law. Now the
works of the flesh are evident, which are: adultery, fornication,
uncleanness, lewdness, idolatry, sorcery, hatred, contentions,
jealousies, outbursts of wrath, selfish ambitions, dissensions, heresies,
envy, murders, drunkenness, revelries, and the like; of which I tell you
beforehand, just as I also told you in time past, that those who practice
such things will not inherit the kingdom of God. But the fruit of the
Spirit is love, joy, peace, longsuffering, kindness, goodness,
faithfulness, gentleness, self–control. Against such there is no law.
And those who are Christ's have crucified the flesh with its passions
and desires. If we live in the Spirit, let us also walk in the Spirit.*

True Liberty

The continual reference over the past years concerning freedom
and liberty has caused these terms to lose much of their original
meaning, especially as they relate to Christianity. The common
definition of liberty, the freedom to do what one wants to please self,
may fit into the attitudes of today's society; however, this concept has
no place among those who have personally accepted Christ as Saviour
and Lord. To the believer, God cries "Stand fast therefore in the liberty
wherewith Christ hath made us free, and be not entangled again with
the yoke of bondage." Through Christ's death and resurrection, the
believer is potentially freed from the power of sin. The Bible says
"Our old self was crucified with Him that our body of sin might be
made powerless, that we should no longer be slaves to sin." (Romans
6:6). We are told "He who raised Christ Jesus from the dead will also
give life to your mortal bodies through His Spirit who indwells
you."(Romans 8:11). Upon receiving Christ as Saviour, each believer
has the Spirit of God within Him and by the Holy Spirit's power; he

has the freedom to do what he should do to please God. This true Christian liberty is expressed in practical Godliness and Christian love.

It is sad to see so many Christians return to bondage by turning liberty into legalism by trying to become 'spiritual' through fulfilling certain rules, or worse yet, by turning their liberty into license and pursuing ungodly pleasures. Dear Christian friend, don't be persuaded by the world's idea of liberty, "Walk by the Spirit and you will not fulfil the lusts of the flesh." (Galatians 5:16).

God intends for the expression of liberty among His own to be the showing of love which always puts the other person's best interests first. To this cause Paul challenged the believers in Rome with these words: "But if thy brother be grieved with [thy] meat, now walkest thou not charitably. Destroy not him with thy meat, for whom Christ died...[It is] good neither to eat flesh, nor to drink wine, nor [any thing] whereby thy brother stumbleth, or is offended, or is made weak" (Romans 14:15,21).

Amy Carmichael in "If" captures the sense of Christian liberty with these thoughts "If I hold on to choices of any kind, just because they are my choices; if I give any room to my private likes and dislikes ... if I put my own happiness before the well-being of the work entrusted to me, I know nothing of Calvary love." Imagine the impact the Christians of the world would have if each lived this truly liberated way!

Personal Notes

John 8: 31-45

Then Jesus said to those Jews who believed Him, "If you abide in My word, you are My disciples indeed. "And you shall know the truth, and the truth shall make you free." They answered Him, "We are Abraham's descendants, and have never been in bondage to anyone. How can you say, 'You will be made free'?"

Jesus answered them, "Most assuredly, I say to you, whoever commits sin is a slave of sin. "And a slave does not abide in the house forever, but a son abides forever. "Therefore if the Son makes you free, you shall be free indeed. "I know that you are Abraham's descendants, but you seek to kill Me, because My word has no place in you. "I speak what I have seen with My Father, and you do what you have seen with your father."

They answered and said to Him, "Abraham is our father."

Jesus said to them, "If you were Abraham's children, you would do the works of Abraham. "But now you seek to kill Me, a Man who has told you the truth which I heard from God. Abraham did not do this. "You do the deeds of your father." Then they said to Him, "We were not born of fornication; we have one Father—God." Jesus said to them, "If God were your Father, you would love Me, for I proceeded forth and came from God; nor have I come of Myself, but He sent Me. "Why do you not understand My speech? Because you are not able to listen to My word. "You are of your father the devil, and the desires of your father you want to do. He was a murderer from the beginning, and does not stand in the truth, because there is no truth in him. When he speaks a lie, he speaks from his own resources, for he is a liar and the father of it. "But because I tell the truth, you do not believe Me.

No Gentle Grafter

In O. Henry's book, 'The Gentle Grafter', the author presents people as easy prey for the con-artist. His stories are often humorous; however, the truth of man's vulnerability cannot be laughed at, especially when eternity is at stake. Scripture tells us that Satan has "blinded the minds of unbelievers, so that they cannot see the light of the glorious gospel of Christ." How true this is. Even in Canada, most people believe that by living a good life, or by obeying the Ten Commandments, or by some other means, they can earn salvation. This is Satan's most successful delusion, because it preys upon the pride of man.

The Bible makes it very clear, man does not deserve heaven, nor can he earn heaven; "For by grace are we saved through faith and that not of ourselves, it is the gift of God, not of works, lest any man should boast." Here scripture states that salvation is by God's grace. Grace implies a favour freely offered, something given yet completely undeserved. Here also, the Bible tells us that salvation is a gift. This implies something given out of love, something certainly unearned.

The only involvement that man has in securing heaven is the response of repentance and faith; repentance that senses sorrow because of sin, and faith that believes Christ paid the penalty of sin on the cross and rose from the dead to certify such claim. Such faith calls on Christ in prayer to be personal Saviour. But what does it say? "The word is near you, in your mouth and in your heart" (that is, the word of faith which we preach): that if you confess with your mouth the Lord Jesus and believe in your heart that God has raised Him from the dead, you will be saved. For with the heart one believes unto righteousness, and with the mouth confession is made unto salvation. For the Scripture says, "Whoever believes on Him will not be put to shame." (Romans 10:8-11).

Satan is no gentle grafter, he is a powerful spirit being opposed to God, who seeks by lies and deception to keep men from the salvation freely offered by a loving Lord. He is not, as some would tell us, a fictitious expression of man's imagination, but a deadly foe, imitating God even to the extent of establishing his own church. Therefore "Be sober, be vigilant; because your adversary the devil, as a roaring lion, walks about, seeking whom he may devour: Whom resist steadfast in the faith" (1 Peter 5:8-9).

Personal Notes

9

1 Corinthians 13:1-8

Though I speak with the tongues of men and of angels, but have not love, I have become sounding brass or a clanging cymbal.
And though I have the gift of prophecy, and understand all mysteries and all knowledge, and though I have all faith, so that I could remove mountains, but have not love, I am nothing.
And though I bestow all my goods to feed the poor, and though I give my body to be burned, but have not love, it profits me nothing.
Love suffers long and is kind; love does not envy; love does not parade itself, is not puffed up; does not behave rudely, does not seek its own, is not provoked, thinks no evil; does not rejoice in iniquity, but rejoices in the truth; bears all things, believes all things, hopes all things, endures all things. Love never fails.

Oasis of the Son

Some people who live in Canada, although they enjoy the beauty of the country, become admittedly weary of the long winter months and look longingly toward a holiday in the sun. There is something refreshing about getting away from the stress of routine busyness and finding an oasis in the warmth of southern sun.

It is that same sense of refreshing that God intended the home to be for its members. However, the busyness of the world has crept in and spoiled the oasis. An article by *Focus on the Family* reported that although fathers say they spent fifteen to twenty minutes with their one year old children, recorded interaction indicated less than one minute of time was being spent. Surveys have indicated that the average public school student in modern North American society watches between four and seven hours of television per day. I have also read recently that of 11,000 teenagers questioned between grades eight and ten, 18% of the girls and 11% of the boys had attempted suicide. There appears to be an absence of any oasis in which many young people can find refreshment and escape from pressure. The home is failing society.

Before giving up on the home, consider this Bible truth: "Except the LORD build the house, they labour in vain that build it: except the LORD keep the city, the watchman waketh [but] in vain." (Psalms 127:1). Scripture states that the home will fail to be the intended oasis if the SON OF GOD never shines there.

Jesus said "I am the light of the world: he that followeth me shall not walk in darkness, but shall have the light of life." (John 8:12). He also said that He would manifest His light in a life surrendered to Him in love: "By this shall all [men] know that ye are my disciples, if ye have love one to another." (John 13:35). It is His love that makes a home an oasis.

The home where that love is a living reality could be described as follows: The home where Christ's love is, suffereth long, [and] is kind; The home where Christ's love is, envieth not; The home where Christ's love is, is not jealous, is not arrogant, Does not behave rudely, seeks not its own, is not easily provoked, keeps no record of wrongs; Rejoices not in evil, but rejoices in the truth; always protects, always trusts, always hopes, always perseveres. The home where Christ's love is, never fails." (1 Corinthians 13). Is your home an Oasis of the Son?

Personal Notes

Matthew 18: 23-35

"Therefore the kingdom of heaven is like a certain king who wanted to settle accounts with his servants. "And when he had begun to settle accounts, one was brought to him who owed him ten thousand talents. "But as he was not able to pay, his master commanded that he be sold, with his wife and children and all that he had, and that payment be made. "The servant therefore fell down before him, saying, 'Master, have patience with me, and I will pay you all.' "Then the master of that servant was moved with compassion, released him, and forgave him the debt. "But that servant went out and found one of his fellow servants who owed him a hundred denarii; and he laid hands on him and took him by the throat, saying, 'Pay me what you owe!' "So his fellow servant fell down at his feet and begged him, saying, 'Have patience with me, and I will pay you all. "And he would not, but went and threw him into prison till he should pay the debt. "So when his fellow servants saw what had been done, they were very grieved, and came and told their master all that had been done. "Then his master, after he had called him, said to him, 'You wicked servant! I forgave you all that debt because you begged me. 'Should you not also have had compassion on your fellow servant, just as I had pity on you?' "And his master was angry, and delivered him to the torturers until he should pay all that was due to him.

Debt Elimination

In 1927 a company in Georgia failed, leaving over five hundred shareholders with worthless stocks. Both the owner of the company and his son vowed to repay the losses. Although the father died relatively poor, twenty-eight years later the son returned the $300,000 in losses. The son was Johnny Mercer, songwriter and singer. He had not forgotten the debt. One of the many songs he wrote that enabled the debt to be paid was "Accentuate the Positive." This seems to be a great way to enter a new year-- get rid of debt and focus on the positive!

It is another Son that brings the greatest meaning to this ambition. Paul emphasises this in the Epistle to the Romans. The severest debt each person must pay is the debt of personal sin: "For all have sinned, and come short of the glory of God;... For the wages of sin [is] death" (Romans 3:23,6:23). Paul reminds us that it was in payment of this debt that Jesus, God's Son died: "But God

12

demonstrates his own love for us in this: While we were still sinners, Christ died for us. Since we have now been justified by his blood, how much more shall we be saved from God's wrath through him!" (Romans 5:8-9 NIV)

Each person's debt of sin and impending wrath from God is declared "paid in full" and "satisfied" respectively by faith in Christ's death, burial and resurrection: "It (righteousness) shall be imputed to us who believe in him who raised Jesus our Lord from the dead. He was delivered over to death for our sins and was raised to life for our justification. Therefore, since we have been justified through faith, we have peace with God through our Lord Jesus Christ" (Romans 4:24-5:1 NIV).

Paul reminds those who believe in Christ that not only is their greatest debt removed--the debt of sin, but that this same faith provides a fresh approach to life--the privilege to view all circumstances through the lens of God's purposes. Paul states: "And we know that in all things God works for the good of those who love him, who have been called according to his purpose." (Romans 8:28 NIV). In this promise, each believer has opportunity to "accentuate the positive" and find complete peace of mind and heart.

With such a fresh start available through this good news about Jesus Christ, it is no wonder that Paul broke out in a song of David: "Blessed are they whose transgressions are forgiven, whose sins are covered. Blessed is the man whose sin the Lord will never count against him." (Romans 4:7-8 from Psalm 32).

May every reader begin this new year sin-debt free and with God's purposes focused through faith in The Son.

Personal Notes

Psalm 47

Oh, clap your hands, all you peoples! Shout to God with the voice of triumph! For the LORD Most High is awesome; He is a great King over all the earth. He will subdue the peoples under us, And the nations under our feet. He will choose our inheritance for us, The excellence of Jacob whom He loves. Selah
God has gone up with a shout, The LORD with the sound of a trumpet. Sing praises to God, sing praises! Sing praises to our King, sing praises! For God is the King of all the earth; Sing praises with understanding. God reigns over the nations; God sits on His holy throne. The princes of the people have gathered together, The people of the God of Abraham. For the shields of the earth belong to God; He is greatly exalted.

Singing to the Lord

Psalm 98 begins with this exhortation: "Sing to the LORD a new song, for he has done marvellous things". The Psalmist urged the people of Israel to rejoice in the goodness of Lord God who had blessed them with the provision of His personal care and salvation. Singing was and continues to be an integral part of the worship of God, especially among the people who know His love. Nevertheless, not all who worship God, know God. This was evident in the life of one of the greatest hymn writers; Fanny Crosby.

Blind from childhood, Fanny was greatly influence by her grandmother. The two enjoyed the world of nature and literature, grandmother sharing in detail the riches of each. Fanny had a great thirst for knowledge and a mind disciplined to work. By the age of ten she had memorized most of the New Testament and over five books of the Old Testament.

Through all her early life Fanny joined in Worship of God. However, it was not until the deaths of several close friends that she understood the true love of God. Deep in her heart, she knew she was not ready to die. On November 20, 1850, Fanny gave her heart to Jesus. Biographer Basil Miller shares her thoughts: "For the first time I realized that I had been trying to hold the world in one hand and the Lord in the other". Charles Stanley in his devotional "In Touch" points out that "the God of her grandmother had become real to her. Her poetry immediately reflected this change in her heart, and songs of praise took the place of regular poems."

Worship today among the people of God is greatly enhanced by the more than 8,500 songs and hymns which Fanny wrote, among them such favourites as "To God be the Glory" and "Tell me the story of Jesus". Every song is a testimony of her love for Jesus Christ.

As this New Year settles in to routine, take a moment to reflect upon the song of your own heart. Is it a song of gloom and despair, a song of loneliness and heartache? God can change the song of any heart by changing the heart itself. Through His provision of salvation you too can "Sing to the LORD a new song, for he has done marvellous things; his right hand and his holy arm have worked salvation for him. The LORD has made his salvation known and revealed his righteousness to the nations."(Psalms 98:1-2 NIV).

Personal Notes

January 7

Romans 3:19-28

Now we know that whatever the law says, it says to those who are under the law, that every mouth may be stopped, and all the world may become guilty before God. Therefore by the deeds of the law no flesh will be justified in His sight, for by the law is the knowledge of sin. But now the righteousness of God apart from the law is revealed, being witnessed by the Law and the Prophets, even the righteousness of God, through faith in Jesus Christ, to all and on all who believe. For there is no difference; for all have sinned and fall short of the glory of God, being justified freely by His grace through the redemption that is in Christ Jesus, whom God set forth as a propitiation by His blood, through faith, to demonstrate His righteousness, because in His forbearance God had passed over the sins that were previously committed, to demonstrate at the present time His righteousness, that He might be just and the justifier of the one who has faith in Jesus. Where is boasting then? It is excluded. By what law? Of works? No, but by the law of faith. Therefore we conclude that a man is justified by faith apart from the deeds of the law.

God's Mountain of Righteousness

There is a mountain so high and vast that no machinery of man could possibly reach its heights or exhaust its resources. I have stood before this mountain, trying to grasp some measure of understanding of the immeasurable riches that are there. I have gazed at this great summit in an attempt to find a description to share with others that would permit minds to grasp hold of the its wonders. I confess that I am at a loss as to where to begin. Even to describe the event as an ant before the C. N. Tower in Toronto is to assume giant proportions for myself and assign minuscule proportions to the mountain.

Nevertheless, this mountain is the theme and hope of man's salvation. This mountain is the focus of the Epistle to the Romans and focal point of Paul's introductory remarks concerning the gospel of Christ: "I am not ashamed of the gospel, because it is the power of God for the salvation of everyone who believes: first for the Jew, then for the Gentile. For in the gospel **a righteousness from God** is revealed, (Romans 1:16-17 NIV).

This mountain is the righteousness of God, God's own uprightness, defined as a conformity to a standard and perfect

16

compliance to a principle. It is the very nature of God's being as the standard and law Himself. This mountain is the rule of God's actions in which He is always true to His perfect nature; God has never, will never, and can never, be wrong or do wrong. This mountain is the character of God's relations. It is the standard by which acceptance into God's presence is based. This is what God demanded of Adam who failed, and what God demands of all men, who also fail. All fail, except Jesus Christ, God's own Son.

There are those who believe a good life will raise an individual to that height. There are those who believe certain rituals, acts of denial, or expressions of remorse could lift man to such heights. Such concepts are foreign to God's declared truth: "for all have sinned and fall short of the glory of God," (Romans 3:23 NIV).

Yet the unique hope of man is that by faith in Christ, God declares individuals to be righteous. In His grace and love, God alone lifts the repentant believer to the top of that mountain by a judicial decree of acquittal. He can do so by the act of imputation in which the believer's guilt of sin is placed upon Christ at the cross and Christ's own righteousness is ascribed to the believer.

Although my mind is too small to grasp all the wonders of the mountain of God's own righteousness, this one thing I can declare, the righteousness of God that condemned when rejected, saves when accepted because "God made him (Christ) who had no sin to be sin for us, so that in him we might become the righteousness of God" (2 Cor. 5:21 NIV). Friend, come to the mountain!

Personal Notes

Romans 5:12-21

Therefore, just as through one man sin entered the world, and death through sin, and thus death spread to all men, because all sinned— (For until the law sin was in the world, but sin is not imputed when there is no law. Nevertheless death reigned from Adam to Moses, even over those who had not sinned according to the likeness of the transgression of Adam, who is a type of Him who was to come. But the free gift is not like the offense. For if by the one man's offense many died, much more the grace of God and the gift by the grace of the one Man, Jesus Christ, abounded to many. And the gift is not like that which came through the one who sinned. For the judgment which came from one offense resulted in condemnation, but the free gift which came from many offenses resulted in justification. For if by the one man's offense death reigned through the one, much more those who receive abundance of grace and of the gift of righteousness will reign in life through the One, Jesus Christ.) Therefore, as through one man's offense judgment came to all men, resulting in condemnation, even so through one Man's righteous act the free gift came to all men, resulting in justification of life. For as by one man's disobedience many were made sinners, so also by one Man's obedience many will be made righteous. Moreover the law entered that the offense might abound. But where sin abounded, grace abounded much more, so that as sin reigned in death, even so grace might reign through righteousness to eternal life through Jesus Christ our Lord.

Biblical Justification

A number of years ago Eugene Joudan of Miami, Florida had the unusual distinction of being number one on America's most unwanted list. Because he had been arrested so many times by mistaken identity with an escaped convict of the same name, Judge Alfonso Sepe ordered pictured posters to be placed in every post office that read: "Do not arrest this man!"

This reminds me of the way in which God's view changes toward the new believer: "Therefore, since we have been justified through faith, we have peace with God through our Lord Jesus Christ," (Romans 5:1 NIV). The term "justified" means to be innocent, faultless, guiltless. It refers to being declared upright and wholly conformed to the will of God. Someone has accurately defined justification as "just-as-if-I'd-never-sinned."

18

God's new view of a believer is emphasised in the great operating principle of the Christian life: "The just shall live by faith" (Romans 1:17). Here believers are a defined people, they are "the just". This is a pronouncement, not an attainment, a declaration of God, based upon the total removal of sin's judgement through the death of Christ.

It must be understood, however, that righteousness, although not a prerequisite of salvation, is its progressive potential. The prophet Jeremiah gives a unique picture of this: "But blessed is the man who trusts in the LORD, whose confidence is in him. He will be like a tree planted by the water that sends out its roots by the stream. It does not fear when heat comes; its leaves are always green. It has no worries in a year of drought and never fails to bear fruit." (Jeremiah 17:7-8 NIV).

With reference to yesterday's remarks about the mountain of God's righteousness, God's changed view of the new believer places him or her on that mountain by faith. From that mountain top the Christian establishes life's roots and grows in the righteousness of God through the Word. From this privileged place, it is the believer's duty to promote growth: "Like newborn babies, crave pure spiritual milk, so that by it you may grow up in your salvation" (1 Peter 2:2 NIV). For this reason Paul urged the believers at Philippi to "work out your own salvation" (Philippians 2:12). Paul used an agricultural and manufacturing term referring to the effort necessary to glean from the earth what the creator has place there.

Being declared "justified" by faith is a privilege afforded to man out of the mercy and grace of God. It also bears the responsibility of pursuing spiritual growth. As a child gets excited about the evident changes on the wall growth chart, every believer should get excited about growing in the Lord. Christian reader, how is your spiritual growth chart progressing?

Personal Notes

19

Galatians 3:6-14

...just as Abraham "believed God, and it was accounted to him for righteousness." Therefore know that only those who are of faith are sons of Abraham. And the Scripture, foreseeing that God would justify the Gentiles by faith, preached the gospel to Abraham beforehand, saying, "In you all the nations shall be blessed." So then those who are of faith are blessed with believing Abraham. For as many as are of the works of the law are under the curse; for it is written, "Cursed is everyone who does not continue in all things which are written in the book of the law, to do them." But that no one is justified by the law in the sight of God is evident, for "the just shall live by faith." Yet the law is not of faith, but "the man who does them shall live by them." Christ has redeemed us from the curse of the law, having become a curse for us (for it is written, "Cursed is everyone who hangs on a tree"), that the blessing of Abraham might come upon the Gentiles in Christ Jesus, that we might receive the promise of the Spirit through faith.

Living Between the Steps.

I read that a university professor was once greatly affected by the apparent conduct of a soldier who was assigned to provide transportation for him. The soldier, upon picking up the professor at the airport, would constantly disappear into the crowd on errands of mercy ---helping a lost child, aiding a lady overburdened with luggage, giving directions to a confused couple. When the professor asked where the soldier learned to live in that manner, the answer stuck for life: "While on duty in Viet Nam my job was to clear mine fields. I saw many of my friends blown up and I never knew whether my next step would be my last. So I just learned to live between the steps. I learned to get everything I could out of the moments between when I picked my foot up and when I put it down. Every step I took was a whole new world, and I guess I've lived that way ever since."

The operating principle of the gospel involves just such an approach to life. The principle is stated in Romans 1:17; "The just shall live by faith." Having previously defined the people called "the just", consider now the distinguished plateau in which they "shall live".

Paul raises the standard of life from its regular manner as defined by the usual word "bios" to one of real meaning defined by the unique word "zao". Where "bios" refers to the duration of life, "zao" speaks of an enjoyment of real life, life worthy of its name, full of vigour and meaning.

This life comes as an instant change to the believer upon initial faith in Christ. Jesus spoke of it in terms of new birth: "I tell you the truth, no one can see the kingdom of God unless he is born again." (John 3:3 NIV) and qualified it as a possession: "For God so loved the world that he gave his one and only Son, that whoever believes in him shall not perish but have eternal life." (John 3:16 NIV).

However, Jesus also made it very clear that this new "life" was a progressive transformation in quality: "I have come that they may have life (zao), and have it more abundantly." (John 10:10). Paul describes this "real living" in terms of complete absorption in Christ: "For to me to live is Christ, and to die is gain." (Philippians 1:21). This was not a sell-out of reality and turning away from society as a hermit but an expression of the deep and satisfying life of knowing Jesus personally and serving him fully, no matter what vocation is ours.

This distinguished plateau of life for a Christian can be the possession of a joy that goes beyond any circumstance (John 15:11) and a peace that passes all understanding (Philippians 4:6-7). It is truly living out life to its fullest between each step. What is life between steps for you?

Personal Notes

Proverbs 16:1-9

The preparations of the heart belong to man, But the answer of the tongue is from the LORD. All the ways of a man are pure in his own eyes, But the LORD weighs the spirits. Commit your works to the LORD, And your thoughts will be established. The LORD has made all for Himself, Yes, even the wicked for the day of doom. Everyone proud in heart is an abomination to the LORD; Though they join forces, none will go unpunished. In mercy and truth Atonement is provided for iniquity; And by the fear of the LORD one departs from evil. When a man's ways please the LORD, He makes even his enemies to be at peace with him. Better is a little with righteousness, Than vast revenues without justice. A man's heart plans his way, But the LORD directs his steps.

Christian Decision Making

Ella Wilcox wrote a poem that reflects the importance of decision making: "One ship drives east, and another west -With the self-same winds that blow; 'Tis the set of the sails and not the gales, - That decides the way we go. Like the winds of the sea are the ways of fate, -As they voyage along through life; 'Tis the will of the soul -That decides its goal, -And not the calm or the strife." ("Bits and Pieces", December 7, 1995.)

For the Christian, all decisions should be based upon the values and will of God as revealed in scripture and confirmed in the heart. The Lord does not want His children make decisions and plans with self-centred interest: "Now listen, you who say, "Today or tomorrow we will go to this or that city, spend a year there, carry on business and make money." Why, you do not even know what will happen tomorrow. What is your life? You are a mist that appears for a little while and then vanishes. Instead, you ought to say, "If it is the Lord's will, we will live and do this or that." (James 4 NIV)

However, too often believers have approached life with this incorrect, fatalistic attitude: "What will be, will be!" You see, God wants His children to plan their lives according to His will. This is achieved in the steps indicated in Proverbs 16. Step One: "Commit thy works unto the LORD, and thy thoughts shall be established." (16:3); Step Two: "A man's heart deviseth his way: but the LORD directeth his steps." (16:9)

First, a Christian should commit all plans to the Lord in prayer. This pray focuses on the goal of the Christian life: "..whatever you do, do it all for the glory of God." (1 Corinthians 10:31 NIV) When plans are bathed in prayer, the Holy Spirit directs the development of plans within the mind and heart in accord with God's Word: "Howbeit when the Spirit of truth, is come, he will guide you into all truth" (John 16:13).

Secondly, as this plan is daily pursued, with continued prayer and direction by the Holy Spirit through the Word of God, the Lord directs the steps. This direction, although it may come through circumstances, or through the advice of other believers, or through presented choices, will always be confirmable by the principles of God's Word: "Thy word [is] a lamp unto my feet, and a light unto my path." (Psalms 119:105).

It is apparent that the "the will of the soul" which determines "the set of the sails" in the Christian life, must be fashioned after the Word of God, in study and prayer. For this reason, let all who know Christ as Saviour, set aside time each day to follow Paul's plea: "Study to shew thyself approved unto God, a workman that needeth not to be ashamed, rightly dividing the word of truth" (2 Timothy 2:15).

Personal Notes

1 Corinthians 12:12-26

For as the body is one and has many members, but all the members of that one body, being many, are one body, so also is Christ. For by one Spirit we were all baptized into one body—whether Jews or Greeks, whether slaves or free—and have all been made to drink into one Spirit. For in fact the body is not one member but many. If the foot should say, "Because I am not a hand, I am not of the body," is it therefore not of the body? And if the ear should say, "Because I am not an eye, I am not of the body," is it therefore not of the body? If the whole body were an eye, where would be the hearing? If the whole were hearing, where would be the smelling? But now God has set the members, each one of them, in the body just as He pleased. And if they were all one member, where would the body be? But now indeed there are many members, yet one body. And the eye cannot say to the hand, "I have no need of you"; nor again the head to the feet, "I have no need of you." No, much rather, those members of the body which seem to be weaker are necessary. And those members of the body which we think to be less honourable, on these we bestow greater honour; and our unpresentable parts have greater modesty, but our presentable parts have no need. But God composed the body, having given greater honour to that part which lacks it, that there should be no schism in the body, but that the members should have the same care for one another. And if one member suffers, all the members suffer with it; or if one member is honoured, all the members rejoice with it.

Unholy Division

One of the most harmful things that has transpired within the church is the division (within the minds of people) of "clergy" and "laity". This division has often interrupted God's purpose of unity and plan for ministry.

God clearly declared an equality among Christians, achieved by the wonder of His own grace, which, through Christ's gift of eternal life has, made each true believer as one: "Here there is no Greek or Jew, circumcised or uncircumcised, barbarian, Scythian, slave or free, but Christ is all, and is in all" (Colossians 3:11 NIV). In John's Revelation of Jesus Christ, there is specific warning against the doctrine of the Nicolaitans. Nevertheless, this practice of oppressing people, which grew within the Roman culture of slavery, expanded within the church to "clergy/laity" division by 500 A.D.

Sadly, in time believers began to see the "Work" of the church as the sole responsibility of "church officials". Christ's prayer was forgotten: "that all of them may be one, Father, just as you are in me and I am in you. May they also be in us so that the world may believe that you have sent me" (John 17:21 NIV), and Christ's intention for the church toward unity and ministry was replaced with human design that failed bring truth to the masses.

How out of line this is with the intention of God, who: "gave some to be apostles, some to be prophets, some to be evangelists, and some to be pastors and teachers, to prepare God's people for works of service, so that the body of Christ may be built up" (Ephesians 4:11-12 NIV).

To each born again believer in Christ, there is a two-fold responsibility: First, there is the responsibility of witness: "..in your hearts set apart Christ as Lord. Always be prepared to give an answer to everyone who asks you to give the reason for the hope that you have. But do this with gentleness and respect," (1 Peter 3:15 NIV). Second, there is the responsibility of service: "Each one should use whatever gift he has received to serve others, faithfully administering God's grace in its various forms" (1 Peter 4:10 NIV).

For each faithful steward there is great promise: "God is not unjust; he will not forget your work and the love you have shown him as you have helped his people and continue to help them" (Hebrews 6:10 NIV). As with faithful Ruth, to each good steward a blessing awaits: "May the LORD repay you for what you have done. May you be richly rewarded by the LORD, the God of Israel, under whose wings you have come to take refuge" (Ruth 2:12 NIV).

May the words of Christ's prayer ring in the ears of all His own: "As you sent me into the world, I have sent them into the world... I in them and you in me. May they be brought to complete unity to let the world know that you sent me and have loved them even as you have loved me" (John 17:18 NIV).

Personal Notes

25

2 Corinthians 4:5-16

For we do not preach ourselves, but Christ Jesus the Lord, and ourselves your bondservants for Jesus' sake. For it is the God who commanded light to shine out of darkness, who has shone in our hearts to give the light of the knowledge of the glory of God in the face of Jesus Christ. But we have this treasure in earthen vessels, that the excellence of the power may be of God and not of us. We are hard pressed on every side, yet not crushed; we are perplexed, but not in despair; persecuted, but not forsaken; struck down, but not destroyed—— always carrying about in the body the dying of the Lord Jesus, that the life of Jesus also may be manifested in our body. For we who live are always delivered to death for Jesus' sake, that the life of Jesus also may be manifested in our mortal flesh. So then death is working in us, but life in you. And since we have the same spirit of faith, according to what is written, "I believed and therefore I spoke," we also believe and therefore speak, knowing that He who raised up the Lord Jesus will also raise us up with Jesus, and will present us with you. For all things are for your sakes, that grace, having spread through the many, may cause thanksgiving to abound to the glory of God. Therefore we do not lose heart. Even though our outward man is perishing, yet the inward man is being renewed day by day.

Standing Fast

In "A View from the Zoo", author Gary Richmond tells about the challenges awaiting the new born giraffe: "The mother giraffe lowers her head long enough to take a quick look. Then she positions herself directly over her calf. She waits for about a minute and then she does the most unreasonable thing, She swings her long, pendulous leg outward and kicks her baby, so that it is sent sprawling head over heels.

When it doesn't get up the violent process is repeated over and over again....Finally, the calf stands for the first time on its wobbly legs. Then the mother giraffe does the most remarkable thing. She kicks it off its feet again. Why? She wants it to remember how to get up. In the wild, baby giraffes must be able to get up as quickly as possible in order to stay with the herd, where there is safety."

There are times when God has to care for His own people in a similar fashion! James reminds us that the Christian is to "Consider it pure joy, my brothers, whenever you face trials of many kinds, because you know that the testing of your faith develops perseverance. Perseverance must finish its work so that you may be mature and complete, not lacking anything" (James 1:2-4 NIV).

Most people would choose to lead a quiet life without trial or hardship. North American society has grown accustomed to relative ease compared to the rest of the world; therefore, it has come to expect such ease as a right. For this reason the hardship of sickness, the trial of poverty, the environment of want, and the presence of death, (circumstances that two-thirds of the world face all their lives), devastate our society.

Into both worlds God sends His own, to reflect the hope and promises of His love. But wells that are never drawn from cannot produce fresh water. Therefore, God sends trial to the believer. Such trials translate hope and promise into living faith that speaks the language of any people or culture.

Should Christians begrudge the temporary suffering of this life that God may call them to, when the very Son of God suffered eternal death and hell for them? Should those with eternal life turn aside from earthly hardship, considering that "God demonstrates his own love for us in this: While we were still sinners, Christ died for us" (Romans 5:8 NIV)?

These trials, when faced in the strength of the Lord, may cause others to find life. Therefore, Christian sufferer, hear the Words of Christ: "If anyone would come after me, he must deny himself and take up his cross and follow me" (Mark 8:34 NIV), and practice the challenge of Peter: "in your hearts set apart Christ as Lord. Always be prepared to give an answer to everyone who asks you to give the reason for the hope that you have. But do this with gentleness and respect," (1 Peter 3:15 NIV). Even those "born again" must learn to stand.

Personal Notes

2 Corinthians 5:14-21

For the love of Christ compels us, because we judge thus: that if One died for all, then all died; and He died for all, that those who live should live no longer for themselves, but for Him who died for them and rose again. Therefore, from now on, we regard no one according to the flesh. Even though we have known Christ according to the flesh, yet now we know Him thus no longer. Therefore, if anyone is in Christ, he is a new creation; old things have passed away; behold, all things have become new. Now all things are of God, who has reconciled us to Himself through Jesus Christ, and has given us the ministry of reconciliation, that is, that God was in Christ reconciling the world to Himself, not imputing their trespasses to them, and has committed to us the word of reconciliation. Now then, we are ambassadors for Christ, as though God were pleading through us: we implore you on Christ's behalf, be reconciled to God. For He made Him who knew no sin to be sin for us, that we might become the righteousness of God in Him.

Blessed are The Peacemakers

Whether it be Ken Taylor helping Americans escape hostilities or Anthony Vincent helping negotiate with commandos holding hostages in Lima, Peru, Canada is on the forefront of peace-making. This not only gives our country a sense of pride, but also a sense of responsibility. However, as much as Canada is often looked to for mediation, true peace-making is more than political persuasion. Even though Canadian leaders have become world renowned for their efforts to bring resolution out of disagreement and reconciliation out of discord among men, true peace-making is a matter of hearts before God.

Jesus said: "Blessed are the peacemakers: for they shall be called the children of God" (Matthew 5:9). Yet this was in the context of inheriting the kingdom of God and hungering and thirsting after righteousness. True peace-making begins with a right relationship between God and man, where reconciliation is made between sinful man and Holy God.

For this purpose Christ went to the cross of Calvary. His death was the provision of reconciliation to all who will believe. Paul said: "Therefore being justified by faith, we have peace with God through our Lord Jesus Christ: By whom also we have access by faith into this grace wherein we stand, and rejoice in hope of the glory of God" (Romans 5:1-2).

To this purpose each Christian is called to be an ambassador: "We are therefore Christ's ambassadors, as though God were making his appeal through us. We implore you on Christ's behalf: Be reconciled to God. God made him who had no sin to be sin for us, so that in him we might become the righteousness of God" (2 Corinthians 5:20-21 NIV).

As this new year commences, it is my prayer that each reader will be reconciled to God for "Everyone who calls on the name of the Lord will be saved." (Romans 10:13), and that each believer will realize the sense of responsibility to be ambassadors for Christ. To this end Paul urges: "Therefore, my dear brothers, stand firm. Let nothing move you. Always give yourselves fully to the work of the Lord, because you know that your labour in the Lord is not in vain" (1 Corinthians 15:58 NIV).

Personal Notes

James 1:2-12

My brethren, count it all joy when you fall into various trials, knowing that the testing of your faith produces patience. But let patience have its perfect work, that you may be perfect and complete, lacking nothing. If any of you lacks wisdom, let him ask of God, who gives to all liberally and without reproach, and it will be given to him. But let him ask in faith, with no doubting, for he who doubts is like a wave of the sea driven and tossed by the wind. For let not that man suppose that he will receive anything from the Lord; he is a double-minded man, unstable in all his ways. Let the lowly brother glory in his exaltation, but the rich in his humiliation, because as a flower of the field he will pass away. For no sooner has the sun risen with a burning heat than it withers the grass; its flower falls, and its beautiful appearance perishes. So the rich man also will fade away in his pursuits. Blessed is the man who endures temptation; for when he has been approved, he will receive the crown of life which the Lord has promised to those who love Him.

The Power of Persistence.

Douglas MacArthur probably would have died in obscurity had it not been for his perseverance. His first attempt at entrance into West Point Military Academy was turned down, his second attempt was also turned down. But MacArthur persisted, was accepted, and became one of the great military leaders of all time. General Douglas MacArthur marched into history books because he learned the power of persistence!

In relating to fellow Christians, Peter encouraged persistence as a valuable character trait: "And beside this, giving all diligence, add to your faith virtue; and to virtue knowledge; And to knowledge temperance; and to temperance patience; and to patience godliness" (2 Peter 1:5-6). Patience in this text is a compound word meaning "to remain under". The term expresses the dual idea of waiting expectantly and standing courageously.

Christians are called to wait expectantly for the promises of God. This was evident in the life of David. While being pursued by King Saul, betrayed Doeg, separated from family, and cut off from the house of the Lord, he patiently declared: "I am still confident of this: I will see the goodness of the LORD in the land of the living. Wait for the LORD; be strong and take heart and wait for the LORD" (Psalms

27 NIV). Like a child waiting for Christmas morning, when all the gifts can be opened and enjoyed, the believer is called to perseverance in trail, to wait expectantly for the goodness of God.

As well, believers are called to stand courageously in the hour of rebuke. Like the apostles, who, having being beaten and told to refrain from sharing the news about the Living Saviour, responded with these words: "Judge for yourselves whether it is right in God's sight to obey you rather than God. For we cannot help speaking about what we have seen and heard" (Acts 4:19-20 NIV), so the Christian must persevere, holding to loyalty to the Lord.

Two frogs fell into a can of cream, or so I've heard it told. The sides of the can were shiny and steep, the cream was deep and cold. "Oh what's the use?" croaked number one, "Tis fate! No help's around. Goodbye my friend, - goodbye sad world!" and weeping still he drowned. But number two, of sterner stuff, dog-paddled in surprise. The while he wiped his creamy face and dried his creamy eyes. "I'll swim awhile at least." he said, or so I've heard he said. "It really will not help the world, if one more frog were dead." An hour or two, he kicked and swam, not once he stopped to mutter, but kicked, and kicked, and swam, and kicked, then hopped out - via butter!"

The thick cream that tries to drown us often becomes the rich butter that lifts us up when, in God's strength, patient persistence is applied. Christian friend, as soldiers of Christ, enter the battles of life with godly persistence.

Personal Notes

Ecclesiastes 12:1-7

Remember now your Creator in the days of your youth, Before the difficult days come, And the years draw near when you say, "I have no pleasure in them": While the sun and the light, The moon and the stars, Are not darkened, And the clouds do not return after the rain; In the day when the keepers of the house tremble, And the strong men bow down; When the grinders cease because they are few, And those that look through the windows grow dim; When the doors are shut in the streets, And the sound of grinding is low; When one rises up at the sound of a bird, And all the daughters of music are brought low; Also they are afraid of height, And of terrors in the way; When the almond tree blossoms, The grasshopper is a burden, And desire fails. For man goes to his eternal home, And the mourners go about the streets. Remember your Creator before the silver cord is loosed, Or the golden bowl is broken, Or the pitcher shattered at the fountain, Or the wheel broken at the well. Then the dust will return to the earth as it was, And the spirit will return to God who gave it.

Creation's Cry

I recently stood beside a nearby lake and gazed upon the blanket of fresh-fallen snow, unmarred by human intrusion and sparkling in the early morning sun. This caused me to marvel at the chosen unbelief of evolutionists who would reduce such splendour to chance when the words of scripture were so vividly realized before my eyes: "For since the creation of the world God's invisible qualities--his eternal power and divine nature--have been clearly seen, being understood from what has been made, so that men are without excuse" (Romans 1:20 NIV). Creation's wonders are a revelation to point fallen man to his need of a restored relationship to his creator. Evolutionists would not only denounce that truth, but deny the very existence of a personal God.

Henry Morris, in his book "War Against God" makes some interesting observations regarding the creation/evolution conflict. He states: "The essence of the everlasting gospel... is that God must be worshipped first of all as creator of all things. That is not all the gospel, of course, for he must also be received as Saviour and Lord, but it is the very foundation of the gospel, and the whole structure collapses without it... The extremely powerful testimony of God in his creation has been corrupted and undermined and almost obliterated in the minds of men by the evolutionary reinterpretation of that testimony.

Nevertheless the evidence is still there, clear and powerful for all whose hearts and minds are willing to see it. Only an omnipotent, omniscient, personal God could possibly account in any rational sense for the evidences of limitless power in the processes of the universe or the infinite complexities of design in the organized systems of the universe (especially living systems!) or the attributes of personality in human beings (self-consciousness, will, emotion, abstract reasoning, etc.). This is the only logical, cause and effect reasoning, which is supposed to be the basic approach to any scientific study of the universe."

Countless books have been written to show evidences on both sides of the conflict: creationists cite detailed geological and mathematical proof, evolutionists cite supposed "missing links." Both arguments are founded upon unprovable presuppositions which require faith either in the Bible account and records, or human assumptions.

However, two things stand out. First, the glory of nature itself shouts "there is a creator." Second, there are still no atheists in foxholes! God, by virtue of created design, put it in man to understand that there is a creator, all nature declares this, the Bible explains this, each person must respond to this. To choose unbelief is death, to choose to believe is to begin the greatest quest of life: to seek, to find and to come to know the living God. To this end, Solomon admonished: "Remember now thy Creator in the days of thy youth, while the evil days come not, nor the years draw nigh, when thou shalt say, I have no pleasure in them" (Ecclesiastes 12:1).

Personal Notes

Psalm 144:9-15

I will sing a new song to You, O God; On a harp of ten strings I will sing praises to You, The One who gives salvation to kings, Who delivers David His servant From the deadly sword. Rescue me and deliver me from the hand of foreigners, Whose mouth speaks lying words, And whose right hand is a right hand of falsehood— That our sons may be as plants grown up in their youth; That our daughters may be as pillars, Sculptured in palace style; That our barns may be full, Supplying all kinds of produce; That our sheep may bring forth thousands And ten thousands in our fields; That our oxen may be well–laden; That there be no breaking in or going out; That there be no outcry in our streets. Happy are the people who are in such a state; Happy are the people whose God is the LORD!

The Source of Happiness

As a new year dawns and most folks try to set some manner of priority and resolutions for their lives, it would seem evident that all would somehow desire to find happiness. As a matter of fact, there is such a quest for happiness that some time ago the NBC television network ran an exposé of the happiness industry in which Maria Shriver interviewed a man from New England that established the "Options Institute." His aim was to become a "happiness coach."

The great problem with such effort is a misunderstanding of true happiness. Those who seek, with conscious effort to find happiness (and most people do), usually associate it with wealth, fame, pleasure, or power, even though history reveals these pursuits to be fruitless in producing happiness. Consider the following testimonies: Lord Byron lived a life of pleasure, if anyone did. He wrote: "The worm, the canker, and the grief are mine alone." Jay Gould, the American millionaire, when dying said: "I suppose I am the most miserable man on earth." Lord Beaconsfield, a man of fortune and fame wrote: "Youth is a mistake; manhood, a struggle; old age, a regret." Alexander the Great conquered the known world in his day. Having done so, he wept stating: "There are no more worlds to conquer."

Where, then, is happiness found? The Bible states the answer: "Happy is the man that findeth wisdom, and the man that getteth understanding" (Proverbs 3:13). With this little word "esher" translated "happiness," God goes far beyond man's definition based

upon the material and the superficial. The word conveys a continuou.
joy, a complete delight, a perfect contentment based upon an
awareness of special favour and unique privilege. This deep,
satisfying, contented "happiness" is only found in the "wisdom and
understanding" that the Lord gives to mankind through His own
revelation - the Word of God: "For the LORD giveth wisdom: out of
his mouth cometh knowledge and understanding" (Proverbs 2:6).

Timothy Dwight in a sermon entitled "The Sovereignty of
God" made this true statement: "Men are merely taller children.
Honour, wealth, and splendour are the toys for which grown children
pine: but which, however accumulated, leave them still disappointed
and unhappy. God never designed that intelligent beings should be
satisfied with these enjoyments. By His wisdom and goodness they
were formed to derive their happiness and virtue form Him alone."

Three pertinent questions arise from this. First, is there belief
that true happiness as defined by God will fulfil a God designed need
within the human heart? Second, is there belief that such happiness
has its source in the wisdom and understanding of God's Word? Third,
if the answer to the first two questions is yes, then will there be a
searching of God's Word rather than a looking to the world for this
true happiness?

"The statutes of the LORD are right, rejoicing the heart...
More to be desired are they than gold, yea, than much fine gold:
sweeter also than honey and the honeycomb" (Psalms 19:8,10).

Personal Notes

Proverbs 3:13-20

Happy is the man that findeth wisdom, and the man that getteth understanding. For the merchandise of it is better than the merchandise of silver, and the gain thereof than fine gold. She is more precious than rubies: and all the things thou canst desire are not to be compared unto her. Length of days is in her right hand; and in her left hand riches and honour. Her ways are ways of pleasantness, and all her paths are peace. She is a tree of life to them that lay hold upon her: and happy is every one that retaineth her. The LORD by wisdom hath founded the earth; by understanding hath he established the heavens. By his knowledge the depths are broken up, and the clouds drop down the dew.

The Suite of Happiness

Doug Whitt and his bride, Sylvia, were escorted to their hotel's bridal suite. They saw a sofa, chairs and table, but where was the bed? Then they discovered the sofa was a hide-a-bed, with a lumpy mattress and sagging springs. They spent a fitful night and woke up in the morning with sore backs. The new husband went to the hotel desk and gave the management a tongue lashing. "Did you open the door in the room?" asked the clerk. Doug went back to the room and opened the door they had thought was a closet. There, complete with fruit baskets and chocolates, was a beautiful bedroom!

Opening all the doors in a honeymoon suite, is like searching all the Words of God. Searching is the door to true happiness: "Happy is the man that findeth wisdom, and the man that getteth understanding" (Prov. 3:13). True happiness is found in God's wisdom. Proverbs 3:14-18 reveals this happiness to be distinct: "For the merchandise of it is better than the merchandise of silver, and the gain thereof than fine gold" (verse 14 - happiness is the true success of a life invested in God's wisdom, where the return is priceless). "She is more precious than rubies: and all the things thou canst desire are not to be compared unto her" (verse 15 - happiness is the true satisfaction of totally fulfilled desires which God's wisdom affords). "Length of days is in her right hand; and in her left hand riches and honour" (verse 16 - happiness is the stability of life founded upon wisdom's riches that are untouched by depreciation or inflation, along with the significance of God's approval gained by wisdom's choices). "Her ways are ways of pleasantness, and all her paths are peace" (verse 17 - happiness is the true security of remaining in wisdom's place of favour and blessing from God, as well as the true safety of wisdom's environment of peace with God). "She is a tree of life to them that lay hold upon her" (verse 18 - happiness is the sustenance of wisdom's nourishment that results in a real fountain of youth, the gift of eternal life through Jesus Christ). Therefore, "happy is every one that retaineth her (wisdom)" (Proverbs 3:18b).

That which men are looking for - success, satisfaction, stability, significance, security, safely, and lasting sustenance, is found only in God. Solomon sought all these in pleasure, power, education and achievement, yet his pursuit led to this plea: "Get wisdom, get understanding: forget it not; neither decline from the words of my mouth. Forsake her not, and she shall preserve thee: love her, and she shall keep thee. Wisdom is the principal thing; therefore, get wisdom: and with all thy getting get understanding. Exalt her, and she shall promote thee: she shall bring thee to honour, when thou dost embrace her. She shall give to thine head an ornament of grace: a crown of glory shall she deliver to thee" (Proverbs 4:5-9).

God's suite of happiness is a door away, open it friend!

Personal Notes

Matthew 11:25-30

At that time Jesus answered and said, "I thank You, Father, Lord of heaven and earth, that You have hidden these things from the wise and prudent and have revealed them to babes. "Even so, Father, for so it seemed good in Your sight. "All things have been delivered to Me by My Father, and no one knows the Son except the Father. Nor does anyone know the Father except the Son, and the one to whom the Son wills to reveal Him. "Come to Me, all you who labour and are heavy laden, and I will give you rest. "Take My yoke upon you and learn from Me, for I am gentle and lowly in heart, and you will find rest for your souls. "For My yoke is easy and My burden is light."

The Big Squeeze

Job lost everything: all his oxen and sheep and all his servants to marauding enemies and fire, and all his children in a tornado, as well as his health to horrible sickness and boils. His crisis was like an unrelenting plague or a never-ending storm. He was squeezed and crushed with unbearable circumstances and although a devout believer and worshipper of the living God, his friends accused him of being rebuked by the Lord for unconfessed sin.

In his agony of soul, Job cried out with bitterness to God. He asked the common questions of men when trial comes: "Why died I not from the womb? (Job 3:11). In essence Job wanted to know why, if God gave him life, did it come with suffering? He asked: Why is light given to a man whose way is hid, and whom God hath hedged in? (Job 3:23). Although here this is a synonym for life, light in the spiritual sense of knowing God suggests Job was asking "Why, if God has brought me to know him, is there no liberty? As well, the continuous nature of Job's suffering caused him to cry out: Why is there no limit? (Job 6:11-13). Job could not understand why his God, who was creator, would not bring him strength and sustenance. Finally, in response to the accusations of his companions, Job asked: Why is there no reprieve of forgiveness if this is of sin? (Job 7:17-21) and Why is there no vindication of he was righteous (Job 10:1-3).

Job, who knew God and lived a conscientious life before his creator, accepting God's provision for sin (Job 1:5), and living in determined obedience (Job 23:11), unburdened his heart to God, sharing his frustrations and anxieties. Although he spoke from his heart with admitted bitterness (Job 30:26) and severe complaint (Job

10:1-3), his faith kept his choices on track. His faith was first expressed in complete trust: "Though he slay me, yet will I trust in him: but I will maintain mine own ways before him" (Job 13:15). No matter what, Job would keep on trusting God. Then his faith was expressed in living hope: "For I know that my redeemer liveth, and that he shall stand at the latter day upon the earth" (Job 19:25). Job understood and anticipated the coming of the Lord to earth to set matters right, he longed to "see His days"(Job 24:1). Finally, faith was expressed in true confidence: "But he knoweth the way that I take: when he hath tried me, I shall come forth as gold" (Job 23:10).

When troubles come and seem never to end, the believer has the privilege to go to God in prayer and unburden his heart; nevertheless, the great path in all circumstances is that often repeated call "The just shall live by faith!" Friend, how do you respond to crisis? Job's path is a sure path, cry out to God with an honest heart, and live by faith: "Come unto me, all ye that labour and are heavy laden, and I will give you rest" (Matthew 11:28).

Personal Notes

John 3:13-21

"No one has ascended to heaven but He who came down from heaven, that is, the Son of Man who is in heaven. "And as Moses lifted up the serpent in the wilderness, even so must the Son of Man be lifted up, "that whoever believes in Him should not perish but have eternal life. "For God so loved the world that He gave His only begotten Son, that whoever believes in Him should not perish but have everlasting life. "For God did not send His Son into the world to condemn the world, but that the world through Him might be saved. "He who believes in Him is not condemned; but he who does not believe is condemned already, because he has not believed in the name of the only begotten Son of God. "And this is the condemnation, that the light has come into the world, and men loved darkness rather than light, because their deeds were evil. "For everyone practicing evil hates the light and does not come to the light, lest his deeds should be exposed. "But he who does the truth comes to the light, that his deeds may be clearly seen, that they have been done in God."

Peace on Earth

A reporter once asked President Herbert Hoover, "Mr. President, how do you handle criticism? Do you ever get agitated or tense?" "No," President Hoover said, seemingly surprised at the question, "of course not."

"But," the reporter went on, "when I was a boy you were one of the most popular men in the world. Then, for a while you became one of the most unpopular, with nearly everyone against you. Didn't any of this meanness and criticism every get under your skin?"

"No, I knew when I went into politics what I might expect, so when it came I wasn't disappointed or upset," he said. He lowered his familiar bushy eyebrows and looked directly into the reporter's eyes. "Besides, I have 'peace at the centre,' you know," he added.

Inner peace comes from God. Peace was the anticipated outcome of Christ's birth according to the angels: "Glory to God in the highest, and on earth peace, good will toward men" (Luke 2:14). Peace is the gift of Jesus Christ. Jesus said: "Peace I leave with you; my peace I give to you."

This inner peace is first, a peace with God, founded upon the finished work of Calvary's cross. There Jesus paid the penalty of man's sin, before Holy God, by shedding His blood in death as a substitute for mankind. Individuals find escape from the death penalty of sin by securing that peace through personal faith in Christ: "Therefore, since we have been justified through faith, we have peace with God through our Lord Jesus Christ... And we rejoice in the hope of the glory of God" (Romans 5 NIV). The new hope is a promised eternity with God.

This inner peace is also the work of the Holy Spirit in a believer which produces a calm resolve and confident trust in any circumstances: "The fruit of the Spirit is love, joy, peace..." (Galatians 5:22). Such peace affords a Christian the capacity to face trial, persecution and even ridicule, with an inner strength of character that responds with love rather than revenge, with care rather than bitterness. This is one of the marks of a maturing Christian.

Several years ago a submarine was being tested and had to remain submerged for many hours. When it returned to the harbour, the captain was asked, "How did the terrible storm last night affect you?" The officer looked at him in surprise and exclaimed, "Storm? We didn't even know there was one!" The sub had been so far beneath the surface that it had reached the area known to sailors as "the cushion of the sea." Although the ocean may be whipped into huge waves by high winds, the waters below are never stirred. The Christian's mind will be protected against the distracting waves of worry and revenge if it is resting completely in the good providence of God. There, sheltered by His grace and encouraged by His Holy Spirit, the believer can find the perfect tranquility that only Christ can provide. Have you His peace?

Personal Notes

2 Peter 3:1-121

Beloved, I now write to you this second epistle (in both of which I stir up your pure minds by way of reminder), that you may be mindful of the words which were spoken before by the holy prophets, and of the commandment of us, the apostles of the Lord and Saviour, knowing this first: that scoffers will come in the last days, walking according to their own lusts, and saying, "Where is the promise of His coming? For since the fathers fell asleep, all things continue as they were from the beginning of creation." For this they willfully forget: that by the word of God the heavens were of old, and the earth standing out of water and in the water, by which the world that then existed perished, being flooded with water. But the heavens and the earth which are now preserved by the same word, are reserved for fire until the day of judgment and perdition of ungodly men. But, beloved, do not forget this one thing, that with the Lord one day is as a thousand years, and a thousand years as one day. The Lord is not slack concerning His promise, as some count slackness, but is longsuffering toward us, not willing that any should perish but that all should come to repentance. But the day of the Lord will come as a thief in the night, in which the heavens will pass away with a great noise, and the elements will melt with fervent heat; both the earth and the works that are in it will be burned up. Therefore, since all these things will be dissolved, what manner of persons ought you to be in holy conduct and godliness, looking for and hastening the coming of the day of God, because of which the heavens will be dissolved, being on fire, and the elements will melt with fervent heat?

Apocalypse When?

There was much speculation and forecast regarding the coming of 2000. Some prophesied apocalyptic doom, others predicted world disaster. At the least, the Y2K bug was to have interrupted much commerce due to computer failure. To the surprise of many, the year came as a great non- event in terms of such speculation. Once again man is proven to be a very poor forecaster of events. This alone points to the absolute wonder of the accuracy of Biblical prophecy. Henry Morris, in "Many Infallible Proofs" makes the following observations regarding the prophecies of Christ's birth:

"... consider the prophecy of Genesis 49:10, in which Jacob, while dying, predicted that Judah would be the one of his twelve sons who would exercise rule over his brethren and from whom the Messiah would come... Next would be the question of where the coming king would be born. Micah predicted it would be in Bethlehem and made his prediction 700 years before it came to pass (Micah 5:2)... But what about predicting the time of Messiah's birth? In Daniel 9:24-26, we have just such a prediction... Although there may be some uncertainty about the exact chronology (some scholars have maintained, quite convincingly, that the fulfilment occurred on the precise day indicated by the prophecy), there can be no reasonable question as to, say, at least the century when it was fulfilled."

"The three prophecies discussed above have a combined probability of chance fulfilment therefore, equal to one out of 12 X 200 X 25, at the very most. This is one chance out of 60,000... And these are only three prophecies out of over 300 that were fulfilled at the first coming of Christ... It seems reasonable to conclude that the phenomenon of fulfilled prophecy constitutes a unique and powerful evidence of the divine inspiration of the Bible."

When considering the complete accuracy of Biblical prophecy in light of apocalyptic predictions, Christ made it clear that no man will know the hour or the day of the end (Matthew 24:36), but the nature of the end is plainly stated: "But the day of the Lord will come like a thief. The heavens will disappear with a roar; the elements will be destroyed by fire, and the earth and everything in it will be laid bare. (2 Peter 3:10 NIV)

To the Christian this prophecy has practical implications for each new day: "But since we belong to the day, let us be self-controlled, putting on faith and love as a breastplate, and the hope of salvation as a helmet. For God did not appoint us to suffer wrath but to receive salvation through our Lord Jesus Christ" (1 Thessalonians 5:8-9 NIV)

The accuracy of Biblical prophecy and the clarity of the nature of earths end constitute a challenge to every believer as a New Millennium Resolution - to live God-centred lives in anticipation of the great day of the Christian home-calling. It is this certainty of fulfilment of prophecy that also calls the unbeliever to turn to the Lord for salvation while time permits: "Today is the day of salvation, tomorrow may not come."

Personal Notes

43

1 Corinthians 15:1-11

Moreover, brethren, I declare to you the gospel which I preached to you, which also you received and in which you stand, by which also you are saved, if you hold fast that word which I preached to you— unless you believed in vain. For I delivered to you first of all that which I also received: that Christ died for our sins according to the Scriptures, and that He was buried, and that He rose again the third day according to the Scriptures, and that He was seen by Cephas, then by the twelve. After that He was seen by over five hundred brethren at once, of whom the greater part remain to the present, but some have fallen asleep. After that He was seen by James, then by all the apostles. Then last of all He was seen by me also, as by one born out of due time. For I am the least of the apostles, who am not worthy to be called an apostle, because I persecuted the church of God. But by the grace of God I am what I am, and His grace toward me was not in vain; but I laboured more abundantly than they all, yet not I, but the grace of God which was with me. Therefore, whether it was I or they, so we preach and so you believed.

The New Jubilee

From the time that Israel first entered the land of promise under the leadership of Joshua and through the 400 years of occupancy under judges and kings, they followed a path of existence that continued as a cycle of obedience and blessing, complacency and sin, hardship and repentance. During this repeated cycle God sought to keep their heart toward Him by loving care as well as loving discipline. In the hard times, when drought and disease, poverty and want became severe, many would sell their inherited land and put their children into slavery, just to "get by."

It was for a reprieve from this slavery and bondage that God established a year of Jubilee every fifty years. This "year of acceptance" would commence with the trumpet call on the day of Atonement and the declaration by the priests of liberating the enslaved and returning land to rightful owners.

Christ came to bring a New Jubilee to the world. He spoke of it in these terms: "The Spirit of the Lord is upon me, because he hath anointed me to preach the gospel to the poor; he hath sent me to heal the broken-hearted, to preach deliverance to the captives, and recovering of sight to the blind, to set at liberty them that are bruised, To preach the acceptable year of the Lord. (Luke 4:18-19). This New Jubilee is the message of "the gospel" that "Christ died for our sins according to the Scriptures, that he was buried, that he was raised on the third day according to the Scriptures" (1 Corinthians 15 NIV) which secures four freedoms:

There is first the FREEDOM FROM THE PAIN of sin which leaves lives crushed and weak emotionally. Christ promises to "heal the broken-hearted." Salvation brings an ever present ministry of the Holy Spirit to secure peace and comfort of heart. Second, there is the FREEDOM FROM THE POWER OF SIN as Christ secures "liberty for the captives." Life without Christ is a slow decent into the enslaving power of sinful habits in which lust, drugs, greed, selfish ambition hold captive the weary soul. As the song testifies: "Christ breaks the power of cancelled sin and sets the prisoner free."

There is also FREEDOM FROM THE PLAGUE OF SIN whereby Christ "gives sight to the blind." Satan, who first deceived Eve, still carries on his campaign of subtle perversion of truth which renders the soul blind. Christ enlightens the spiritual sight, bringing discernment of God's purposes and plans through the illuminating ministry of the Holy Spirit.

Finally, this New Jubilee is FREEDOM FROM THE PATH OF SIN that keeps men in a state of immobility. Christ brings "liberty to the oppressed" by working a confident faith that learns "I can do all things through Christ who strengthens me" (Philippians 4:13).

Christ's New Jubilee is the great work of liberation secured for all who accept the gospel message of Christ's substitutional death for sins and victorious resurrection. Have you responded to the call to enter into Christ's Jubilee?

Personal Notes

Proverbs 23:17-26

*Do not let your heart envy sinners, But be zealous for the fear of the
LORD all the day; For surely there is a hereafter, And your hope will not
be cut off. Hear, my son, and be wise; And guide your heart in the way.
Do not mix with winebibbers, Or with gluttonous eaters of meat;
For the drunkard and the glutton will come to poverty, And drowsiness
will clothe a man with rags. Listen to your father who begot you, And do
not despise your mother when she is old. Buy the truth, and do not sell it,
Also wisdom and instruction and understanding. The father of the
righteous will greatly rejoice, And he who begets a wise child will
delight in him. Let your father and your mother be glad, And let her who
bore you rejoice. My son, give me your heart, And let your eyes observe
my ways.*

The Heart of the Matter

A. W. Tozer said: "The widest thing in the universe is not space;
it is the potential capacity of the human heart. Being made in the image
of God, it is capable of almost unlimited extension in all directions. And
one of the world's greatest tragedies is that we allow our hearts to shrink
until there is room in them for little beside ourselves."

The heart, particularly in Biblical poetry, is that inner part of man
which constitutes his spirit and soul and frames his mind, inclinations,
and emotions. In scriptural language, the heart is the "real you." Tozer's
use of "heart" not only paralleled the biblical term, it also accurately
portrayed the biblical description.

There are four distinct heart conditions suggested in the book of
Proverbs. There is the dying heart, contrasted with the living heart, and
there is the troubled heart contrasted with the triumphant heart. These
summarize the conditions of man's real self and form a pattern for good
self-analysis.

Consider the dying heart in contrast to the living. The dying heart
is described as contemptuous, provoked toward God as a result of His
ordering of circumstances intended to bring correction (Proverbs 5:12).
The dying heart is also perverse, twisting God's Word and distorting
truth (11:20). It is hardened toward God (28:14), foolish (12:23), and
wicked (26:23).

The living heart trusts in the Lord no matter what circumstances
come (Proverbs 3:5). The living heart is discerning, understanding the
grace and mercy of God (8:5). It is a heart that fears (reverences) the

46

Lord in all of life's pursuits and activities. The living heart searches for the wisdom of God as revealed in Scripture and seeks to live accordingly. It is, therefore, a prudent heart (16:21). Finally, the living heart is a pure heart (22:11), not by any virtue of its own, but by the grace of God that forgives sin and changes the inner man.

The difference between the dying heart and the living heart is relationship to God. Scripture reveals that the "real you" of every person is born apart from God and kept apart by sin. It is not religion or efforts to make up for sin, that remedies the state of man's heart, it is relationship. Proverbs states it in terms of a surrendered heart: "My son, give me thine heart, and let thine eyes observe my ways" (Proverbs 23:26). Christ spoke of this in terms of new birth: "Verily, verily, I say unto thee, Except a man be born again, he cannot see the kingdom of God" (John 3:3). Both refer to the believing choice of surrendering "the real you" to God: "That if thou shalt confess with thy mouth the Lord Jesus, and shalt believe in thine heart that God hath raised him from the dead, thou shalt be saved. For with the heart man believeth unto righteousness; and with the mouth confession is made unto salvation" (Romans 10:9-10).

Such a choice of faith delivers a person from a dying heart, and grants a living heart (Ephesians 2:1). Friend, how is your heart condition?

Personal Notes

Job 24:1-12

"Since times are not hidden from the Almighty, Why do those who know Him see not His days? "Some remove landmarks; They seize flocks violently and feed on them; They drive away the donkey of the fatherless; They take the widow's ox as a pledge. They push the needy off the road; All the poor of the land are forced to hide. Indeed, like wild donkeys in the desert, They go out to their work, searching for food. The wilderness yields food for them and for their children. They gather their fodder in the field And glean in the vineyard of the wicked. They spend the night naked, without clothing, And have no covering in the cold. They are wet with the showers of the mountains, And huddle around the rock for want of shelter. "Some snatch the fatherless from the breast, And take a pledge from the poor. They cause the poor to go naked, without clothing; And they take away the sheaves from the hungry. They press out oil within their walls, And tread winepresses, yet suffer thirst. The dying groan in the city, And the souls of the wounded cry out; Yet God does not charge them with wrong.

The Groaning Heart

For many, looking back on the previous is a matter of counting blessings and enjoying fond memories. However, there are others who look back to a single wave of destruction that passed as a blur, leaving only the sense of loss. For some, this has been a year of disaster. These are people who understand, by personal experience, the depth of feeling behind Job's words "Men groan from out of the city, and the soul of the wounded crieth out." (Job 24:12)

The word "groan" comes from a term that means pierced or stabbed and refers to a person who has been wounded of heart. Job certainly qualified, yet in his cry, his associates responded with callused hearts and sharp tongues. Those he thought to be friends failed him in his time of need.

Today many hearts have been pierced with loss, and like Job, cry out only to find rebuke and accusation as answer to their hurt. Yet there is reason for hope. In the story of Job we are reminded that God never abandons those who put their trust in him: "the LORD blessed the latter end of Job more than at the beginning" (Job 42:12). To all who will trust in God, he proves to be that special friend that sticks closer than a brother (Proverbs 18:24).

David knew where to look for help: "I will lift up my eyes to the hills--From whence comes my help? My help comes from the LORD, Who made heaven and earth. He will not allow your foot to be moved; He who keeps you will not slumber... The LORD is your keeper" (Psalm 121).

For all those hearts that have been pierced groan within, there is hope for healing! Through the love that led Him to die for us and the power that raised Him from death, Jesus secured the restoration of the whole man. He alone can truthfully say "The Spirit of the Lord [is] upon me, because he hath anointed me to preach the gospel to the poor; he hath sent me to heal the brokenhearted, to preach deliverance to the captives, and recovering of sight to the blind, to set at liberty them that are bruised" (Luke 4:18). He, as a true friend that loves at all times, never turns a deaf ear nor cold shoulder to those who cry in pain for His help. In turning to Him man is encouraged to lay their cares and hurts at his feet, because he truly cares for each soul(1 Peter 5:7). Perhaps James Small penned this best when he wrote this hymn stanza: "I've found a friend, O such a Friend! He loved me ere I knew Him; He drew me with the cords of love and thus He bound me to Him. And round my heart still closely twine those ties which naught can sever, for I am His and He is mine, forever and forever." This friend that Job and James found desires to be your friend as well. Will you make him so?

Personal Notes

Isaiah 11:12-12:6

He will set up a banner for the nations, And will assemble the outcasts of Israel, And gather together the dispersed of Judah From the four corners of the earth. Also the envy of Ephraim shall depart, And the adversaries of Judah shall be cut off; Ephraim shall not envy Judah, And Judah shall not harass Ephraim. But they shall fly down upon the shoulder of the Philistines toward the west; Together they shall plunder the people of the East; They shall lay their hand on Edom and Moab; And the people of Ammon shall obey them. The LORD will utterly destroy the tongue of the Sea of Egypt; With His mighty wind He will shake His fist over the River, And strike it in the seven streams, And make men cross over dry–shod. There will be a highway for the remnant of His people Who will be left from Assyria, As it was for Israel In the day that he came up from the land of Egypt.

And in that day you will say: "O LORD, I will praise You; Though You were angry with me, Your anger is turned away, and You comfort me. Behold, God is my salvation, I will trust and not be afraid; 'For YAH, the LORD, is my strength and song; He also has become my salvation.'" Therefore with joy you will draw water From the wells of salvation. And in that day you will say: "Praise the LORD, call upon His name; Declare His deeds among the peoples, Make mention that His name is exalted. Sing to the LORD, For He has done excellent things; This is known in all the earth. Cry out and shout, O inhabitant of Zion, For great is the Holy One of Israel in your midst!"

Satisfaction

Each morning at the time of the sacrifice during the seven days of the feast a priest proceeded to the fountain of Siloah with a golden pitcher. He filled it with water and, accompanied by a solemn procession, bore it to the alter of burnt sacrifice, pouring the water, together with the contents of a pitcher of wine from the drink offering, into two perforated flat bowls. The trumpets sounded, and the people sang Isaiah 12:3 "Therefore with joy shall ye draw water out of the wells of salvation."

Into that scene entered Jesus with an invitation that stands to this day: "In the last day, that great day of the feast, Jesus stood and cried, saying, If any man thirst, let him come unto me, and drink. He that believeth on me, as the scripture hath said, out of his belly shall flow rivers of living water " (John 7:37-38). This is an invitation to satisfaction, an invitation to find Jesus, the Son of God, as the source and sustainer of eternal life. This eternal life is not a form of experience separate from other experiences, rather, it is the transformation of the whole of life experience. So radical a transformation is the receiving of eternal life that Jesus described it as being "born again."

This wonderful transformation takes place upon faith in Jesus as personal Saviour: "For God so loved the world, that he gave his only begotten Son, that whosoever believeth in him should not perish, but have everlasting life" (John 3:16). The result of that transformation is the Holy Spirit taking up residence in the believer, providing an "on the scene" ministry of comfort, care, guidance and encouragement, and building into the life of a believer the true character of God: "...the fruit of the Spirit is love, joy, peace, longsuffering, kindness, goodness, faithfulness, gentleness, self-control." Nothing brings greater satisfaction in life than the "flowing water" of the ministry of God's Spirit in life.

The Amazon River is the largest river in the world. The mouth is 90 miles across. There is enough water to exceed the combined flow of the Yangtze, Mississippi, and Nile Rivers. So much water comes from the Amazon that they can detect its currents 200 miles out in the Atlantic Ocean. One irony of ancient navigation is that sailors in ancient times died for lack of water--caught in windless waters of the South Atlantic. They were adrift, helpless, dying of thirst. Sometimes other ships from South America who knew the area would come alongside and call out, "What is your problem?" And they would exclaim, "Can you spare us some water? Our sailors are dying of thirst!" And from the other ship would come the cry, "just lower your buckets. You are in the mouth of the mighty Amazon River."

The irony of ancient Israel and the tragedy around us today is that God, the fountain of living water, is right here and people fail to recognize Him! Have you?

Personal Notes

Ezekiel 36:22-30

"Therefore say to the house of Israel, 'Thus says the Lord GOD: "I do not do this for your sake, O house of Israel, but for My holy name's sake, which you have profaned among the nations wherever you went. "And I will sanctify My great name, which has been profaned among the nations, which you have profaned in their midst; and the nations shall know that I am the LORD," says the Lord GOD, "when I am hallowed in you before their eyes. "For I will take you from among the nations, gather you out of all countries, and bring you into your own land. "Then I will sprinkle clean water on you, and you shall be clean; I will cleanse you from all your filthiness and from all your idols. "I will give you a new heart and put a new spirit within you; I will take the heart of stone out of your flesh and give you a heart of flesh. "I will put My Spirit within you and cause you to walk in My statutes, and you will keep My judgments and do them. "Then you shall dwell in the land that I gave to your fathers; you shall be My people, and I will be your God. "I will deliver you from all your uncleannesses. I will call for the grain and multiply it, and bring no famine upon you. "And I will multiply the fruit of your trees and the increase of your fields, so that you need never again bear the reproach of famine among the nations.

Lord Change Me

The passing of a year brings a time of introspection, and often dissatisfaction. That New Year 'look in the mirror' often reveals things we would prefer not to see. When the Edmonton Oilers' centreman Shaun Van Allen had suffered a concussion he temporarily did not know who he was. His coach Ted Green, upon being told of his player's condition replied: "Good, tell him he is Wayne Gretzky." Like the coach, we often wish that we could be someone else, or at the least, be like someone else. The desired changes to our character flaws are too slow in coming!

Scripture attests to the need of man to undergo change. Man, who was originally created in the image of God, suffered severe "image marring" as a result of original sin: "Wherefore, as by one man sin entered into the world, and death by sin; and so death passed upon all men, for that all have sinned" (Romans 5:12). The entire beauty of the image of God in man was corrupted. This image marring scars every person with character flaws as well as death. The uniqueness of true Christian faith is that God the Creator, begins at salvation to recreate that image through Spirit empowered change: "But we all, with open

52

face beholding as in a glass the glory of the Lord, are changed into the same image from glory to glory, even as by the Spirit of the Lord." (2 Corinthians 3:18).

God's promise to the believer is the restoration of his own image. "Now the God of peace, that brought again from the dead our Lord Jesus... Make you perfect in every good work to do his will, working in you that which is well-pleasing in his sight (Hebrews 13:20). This change does not come through demonstrations of the outpouring of God's power as some are prone to seek, but from the quiet, steady walk with the creator Himself: "I am the vine, you are the branches. He who abides in Me, and I in him, bears much fruit; for without Me you can do nothing." (John 15:2). Change is from fellowshipping with God and with those who are also walking with Christ and enjoying His changing influence.

From the beginning of man's creation, God's desire has been to fellowship with him. God walked with Adam and Eve in the garden of Eden prior to their fall into sin (Genesis 3:8). Enoch "walked with God", Abraham was a friend of God, David was a man after God's own heart. The coming of Christ was "Immanuel – God with us." It is God's desired fellowship with man that brought about the avenue of forgiveness through the sacrifice of Christ on the cross, and it is that potential of fellowship, when forgiveness is secured by faith, that promises an intimacy with God which changes lives day by day. Friend, don't despair of what you see in the mirror, put your faith in Christ and allow Him to recreate His own beauty in you.

Personal Notes

John 14:18-29

"I will not leave you orphans; I will come to you. "A little while longer and the world will see Me no more, but you will see Me. Because I live, you will live also. "At that day you will know that I am in My Father, and you in Me, and I in you. "He who has My commandments and keeps them, it is he who loves Me. And he who loves Me will be loved by My Father, and I will love him and manifest Myself to him." Judas (not Iscariot) said to Him, "Lord, how is it that You will manifest Yourself to us, and not to the world?" Jesus answered and said to him, "If anyone loves Me, he will keep My word; and My Father will love him, and We will come to him and make Our home with him. "He who does not love Me does not keep My words; and the word which you hear is not Mine but the Father's who sent Me. "These things I have spoken to you while being present with you. "But the Helper, the Holy Spirit, whom the Father will send in My name, He will teach you all things, and bring to your remembrance all things that I said to you. "Peace I leave with you, My peace I give to you; not as the world gives do I give to you. Let not your heart be troubled, neither let it be afraid. "You have heard Me say to you, 'I am going away and coming back to you.' If you loved Me, you would rejoice because I said, 'I am going to the Father,' for My Father is greater than I. "And now I have told you before it comes, that when it does come to pass, you may believe.

Encouragement

Maggie Kuhn, head of the Grey Panthers, tells of an interesting fact about sand hill cranes. All during the time one bird is leading, the rest are honking, signaling their affirmation. From sand hill cranes we learn the value of encouragement. Yet mankind with its self-centered interest, regularly fails in this business of encouragement, leaving many of its own with a sense of despair and loneliness. Christians have no better record. Sadly, the church is often a place of discouragement rather than encouragement, leaving many to agree with Asher Ben Jehiel, who, nearly 700 years ago, said "Don't rely on the broken reed of human support."

The New Testament word most often translated "encourage" portrays a picture like the one presented by the sand hill cranes. The word is *"parakaleo"* and suggests a drawing close for the purpose of encouragement, comfort, or instruction. Yet the certainty of Christian encouragement does not come from fellow believers but from God himself by way of His Holy Spirit. Jesus promised: 'I will pray the

Father, and he shall give you another *Comforter*, that he may abide with you forever, even the Spirit of truth... for he dwells with you, and shall be in you." (John 14:16-17).

The ministry of God's Holy Spirit is one of encouragement, of drawing close to every believer's heart with expressions of affirmation. This affirmation comes from a God-given sense of the unifying work of His love and labour among His people. The Holy Spirit brings this "sense" through the light of God's Word: "hearts may be *encouraged*, being knit together in love, and attaining to all riches of the full assurance of understanding, to the knowledge of the mystery of God" (Colossians 2:2).

The self-sacrificial love of God, produced in the heart of a believer, overcomes man's tendency toward self-centeredness, liberating a Christian to truly act in the best interests of others. Such actions in turn bind God's people together with the wonder of family care and comfort. This encouraging love was evidenced in the early church, and can be seen today in churches that yield to Christ's sovereign control and headship.

As well, God, through the Holy Spirit, builds understanding of Himself, His ways and the work He is doing around the believer. Here a deepening sense of awe toward God is felt. This in turn produces a spiritual confidence or assurance of God's continuing care and successful rule, bringing great encouragement.

"Mary was having a tough day and moaned to her mom and brother, "Nobody loves me -- the whole world hates me!" Her brother, busily occupied playing a game, hardly looked up at her and passed on this encouraging word: "That's not true, Mary. Some people don't even know you."

Unlike this insensitive brother, God encourages His own by giving them a special blessing; the sense that He Himself knows them, is with them, and willing to reveal more of Himself each day! Need encouragement? - look to Christ, he never fails! (1 Corinthians 13).

Personal Notes

55

1 John 2:7-17

Brethren, I write no new commandment to you, but an old commandment which you have had from the beginning. The old commandment is the word which you heard from the beginning. Again, a new commandment I write to you, which thing is true in Him and in you, because the darkness is passing away, and the true light is already shining. He who says he is in the light, and hates his brother, is in darkness until now. He who loves his brother abides in the light, and there is no cause for stumbling in him. But he who hates his brother is in darkness and walks in darkness, and does not know where he is going, because the darkness has blinded his eyes. I write to you, little children, Because your sins are forgiven you for His name's sake. I write to you, fathers, Because you have known Him who is from the beginning. I write to you, young men, Because you have overcome the wicked one. I write to you, little children, Because you have known the Father. I have written to you, fathers, Because you have known Him who is from the beginning. I have written to you, young men, Because you are strong, and the word of God abides in you, And you have overcome the wicked one. Do not love the world or the things in the world. If anyone loves the world, the love of the Father is not in him. For all that is in the world—the lust of the flesh, the lust of the eyes, and the pride of life—is not of the Father but is of the world. And the world is passing away, and the lust of it; but he who does the will of God abides forever.

Divine Oxygen

It was Sir Walter Raleigh who wrote: "I wish I loved the Human Race; I wish I loved its silly face; I wish I liked the way it walks; I wish I liked the way it talks; And when I'm introduced to one I wish I thought WHAT JOLLY FUN!" Much of humanity is very unlovable. God sees the inner being of every person and declares "The heart is deceitful above all things and desperately wicked" (Jeremiah 17:9). Nevertheless, God sees beyond this ugly heart of sin and selfishness to the need. God's Word declares: "God demonstrated His love toward us in that while we were yet sinners, Christ died for us." (Rom. 5:8). To accept Christ as Saviour is to accept the love of God and a new capacity to love humanity.

Roger Thompson, in *Leadership Magazine*, made this observation: "Ever feel overwhelmed by the Bible's command to love unconditionally? When people ask me, "How can I ever start to love everyone like I should?" I give the same answer I give those who ask how they can start jogging: Start slow, and then get slower! For the first week, the goal is "just to keep moving." Too many people buy new shoes and a fancy running suit and sprint out the door, eagerly chugging as hard as they can for about three blocks. Then their stomachs begin to ache, their muscles cramp, and their lungs burn. They wind up hitchhiking home exhausted, and gasp, "I will never do that again." That's called anaerobic (without oxygen) running. It's caused by a body using up more oxygen than it takes in. Many people try to run that way, and many people try to love that way. They love with great fervor and self-sacrifice, giving 100 percent but without the resources to continue for a lifetime. Down the road they find themselves in pain, gasping and cramped, saying, "I will never do that again." Love, like running, must be aerobic.

Our output must be matched by our intake. Running requires oxygen. An enduring love requires God's word, his consolation, his presence. As we love aerobically, we'll build up our capacity to do more and more. And pretty soon we won't be huffing and puffing for half a mile; we'll be running marathons. The key to loving people is to love God. In loving God, we are drawn close to Him and gain the perspective of His love toward the world. It was Christ who could say, while hanging from Calvary's cross "Forgive them, for they know not what they do." It was Christ's love in Stephen that prompted him to say at the hands of his own murderers "Forgive them." It is Christ's love in the believer that wins the marathons by the "oxygen" of His grace, and that oxygen never runs out!

Friend, like Sir Walter Raleigh, are you struggling with loving cruel and crude humanity? Start with Christ's love for you, and get a second breath for the race.

Personal Notes

Genesis 3:1-13

Now the serpent was more cunning than any beast of the field which the LORD God had made. And he said to the woman, "Has God indeed said, 'You shall not eat of every tree of the garden'?" And the woman said to the serpent, "We may eat the fruit of the trees of the garden; "but of the fruit of the tree which is in the midst of the garden, God has said, 'You shall not eat it, nor shall you touch it, lest you die.'" Then the serpent said to the woman, "You will not surely die. "For God knows that in the day you eat of it your eyes will be opened, and you will be like God, knowing good and evil." So when the woman saw that the tree was good for food, that it was pleasant to the eyes, and a tree desirable to make one wise, she took of its fruit and ate. She also gave to her husband with her, and he ate. Then the eyes of both of them were opened, and they knew that they were naked; and they sewed fig leaves together and made themselves coverings. And they heard the sound of the LORD God walking in the garden in the cool of the day, and Adam and his wife hid themselves from the presence of the LORD God among the trees of the garden. Then the LORD God called to Adam and said to him, "Where are you?" So he said, "I heard Your voice in the garden, and I was afraid because I was naked; and I hid myself." And He said, "Who told you that you were naked? Have you eaten from the tree of which I commanded you that you should not eat?" Then the man said, "The woman whom You gave to be with me, she gave me of the tree, and I ate." And the LORD God said to the woman, "What is this you have done?" The woman said, "The serpent deceived me, and I ate."

Humanity in Pieces

Although war continued for years, it took the horror of a terrorist attack on America to wake the world up to the overwhelming devastation of evil dictatorship. It would seem that unless humanity sees itself in pieces it assumes all is well! This can also be said for the state of destruction that the family is in. The perfect paradise of Genesis chapter two was viciously torn apart by Satan who introduced sin and rebellion.

Satan, in his own pride-induced rebellion against God (see Isaiah 14:12-15), carried that rebellion into paradise by usurping the authority of God's Word: "He said to the woman, "Did God really say, 'You must not eat from any tree in the garden'?....You will not surely die, for God knows that when you eat of it your eyes will be opened, and you will be like God, knowing good and evil." (Genesis 3:4-5 NIV).

Satan turned Adam and Eve's God-created desire for food and wisdom, within a perfect plan, to personal lust outside of God's will. "When the woman saw that the fruit of the tree was good for food and pleasing to the eye, and also desirable for gaining wisdom, she took some and ate it. She also gave some to her husband, who was with her, and he ate it." (Genesis 3:6 NIV).

Paradise was destroyed, only devastation remained. Genesis 3:7-12 records the devastation; beautiful intimacy became shameful nakedness, perfect harmony became selfish discord, meaningful fellowship with God became fear before God. In that single act of rebellion, the parents of humanity condemned all mankind to death. "Therefore, just as sin entered the world through one man, and death through sin, and in this way death came to all men, because all sinned" (Romans 5:12 NIV).

God's judgment of death was evident: in sin Adam and Eve knew spiritual death, they were separated from God. They knew social death, they were estranged from each other; they would know physical death as their bodies ceased to rejuvenate themselves. Here is mankind's first picture of itself in pieces. Bitter was the taste of sin, great was its destruction!

The resultant judgment upon the original family was cushioned in part by God's own initiative to restore fellowship. Although paradise was forfeited, all was not lost. By offering animal skins for Adam and Eve (Genesis 3:21), God indicated the final sacrifice He would provide in His Son: "Christ....has appeared once for all at the end of the ages to do away with sin by the sacrifice of himself. (Hebrews 9:26 NIV).

Even as God restored Adam and Eve to fellowship, He can through Jesus Christ, restore people today. Here are the words of one restored family put to song: "Heartaches, broken pieces, ruined lives are why You died on Calvary; Your touch was what I longed for, you have given life to me." (Gloria and William Gaither).

Personal Notes

Deuteronomy 6:4-12

"Hear, O Israel: The LORD our God, the LORD is one! "You shall love the LORD your God with all your heart, with all your soul, and with all your strength. "And these words which I command you today shall be in your heart. "You shall teach them diligently to your children, and shall talk of them when you sit in your house, when you walk by the way, when you lie down, and when you rise up. "You shall bind them as a sign on your hand, and they shall be as frontlets between your eyes. "You shall write them on the doorposts of your house and on your gates. "So it shall be, when the LORD your God brings you into the land of which He swore to your fathers, to Abraham, Isaac, and Jacob, to give you large and beautiful cities which you did not build, "houses full of all good things, which you did not fill, hewn–out wells which you did not dig, vineyards and olive trees which you did not plant—when you have eaten and are full— "then beware, lest you forget the LORD who brought you out of the land of Egypt, from the house of bondage.

God's Word

In Bible times, ages before the industrial revolution, the tools of trade and the weapons of war had one thing in common: they all operated with the power and/or guidance of human hands. Efficiency was directly related to personal skill and the keenness of the instruments. Every family had first-hand knowledge of the use of the sharpening stone, or "whetstone." The hours spent in repeatedly honing tools or weapons to a fine edge always "paid off" as work or wars were entered upon.

As Moses gave instruction to Israel regarding the character of the family blessed of God (Deuteronomy 6:4-9), he made reference to this very process of repeated sharpening for precision: "These commandments that I give you today are to be upon your hearts. Impress them on your children. Talk about them when you sit at home and when you walk along the road, when you lie down and when you get up."

Although missed in the English translation, the Hebrew word translated "impress" or teach is "Shanan," the word for setting or sharpening. With this word, God emphasized the process and passion involved in teaching His truth in the home. The process was understood as a need for repeated discussion (talk), in which God's Truth, having first been internalized in parents' hearts with fondness, would be related to every aspect of family life (when you sit...walk...lie down...get up). The passion was understood with the sense of urgency suggested by this word, an urgency evident in the importance of sharpening the weapons because the enemy was just over the hill.

The great failure of today's families is the delegation of teaching which formulates our children's values, choices, purposes, and aspirations, to institutions and influences outside the home. In the chapter entitled "The High Call of Parenting," Bill Hybels' book *Honest to God* states: "In the 1940's, the top offenses committed by public school students were talking, chewing gum, making noises, running in the halls... In 1982, the top offenses had changed. They had become rape, robbery, assault, burglary, arson... A million hours of television have made kids talk like valley girls, dress like rock stars, and think like game show contestants."

God has never delegated the responsibility of teaching life values to the government, nor the public school, nor the church school, and certainly not the media. He places the responsibility squarely on the parents: "Train a child in the way he should go, and when he is old he will not turn from it." (Proverbs 22:6 NIV), "Fathers, do not exasperate your children; instead, bring them up in the training and instruction of the Lord." (Ephesians 6 NIV). God's Word is described as a two-edged sword (Hebrews 4:12), and is "useful for teaching, rebuking, correcting and training in righteousness." (2 Timothy 3:16 NIV). How keenly honed is His Sword in your home?

Personal Notes

Psalm 119:9-16 "Beth"

How can a young man cleanse his way? By taking heed according to Your word. With my whole heart I have sought You; Oh, let me not wander from Your commandments! Your word I have hidden in my heart, That I might not sin against You! Blessed are You, O LORD! Teach me Your statutes! With my lips I have declared All the judgments of Your mouth. I have rejoiced in the way of Your testimonies, As much as in all riches. I will meditate on Your precepts, And contemplate Your ways. I will delight myself in Your statutes; I will not forget Your word.

The Word of God is a Love Letter

I remember fumbling through a short story to give to my "sweetheart" while we were dating. I believed the story would express my feelings toward her; nevertheless, considering the fact that she was a school teacher and I had a knack for breaking every grammatical rule in the English language, this was a bold and risky step. I'm sure she must have had quite a chuckle reading this story (no doubt with red correcting pen in hand); however, to my knowledge she still has the story tucked away in some private place kept for her eyes only. As for me, the risk was worth it, my sweetheart has been my wife for twenty-two years.

Whatever form language takes: personal letters, telephone calls, special cards, whispered poems, even silly short stories, most couples cherish that communication with such a special sense of fondness that the letters and cards are often kept for life. It is this kind of "fondness for communication from God" that Moses spoke of when sharing the marks of a home blessed by God: "Love the Lord your God with all your heart and with all your soul and with all your strength. These commandments that I give you today are to be upon your hearts." (Deuteronomy 6:5-6 NIV).

The commandments of God were to be an affair of the heart, not merely of memory. The phrase "upon your heart" suggests that God's word should positively influence our lives in choices and values even as the weight of burdens on our hearts influences us negatively. Christ stated this same truth: "Take my yoke upon you and learn from me, for I am gentle and humble in heart, and you will find rest for your souls." (Matthew 11:29 NIV). To learn from Him is to embrace all His truth as our own; His cross, His path, His will.

Each of these passages reflect the deep fondness and special place that the communication of one greatly loved has in our life. The one loved is the Lord, the love language held so dearly is His Word, the Bible. Helen Frazee-Bower captures that fondness in her poem "I Hold the Book":

> Here in my hands I hold the Holy Book.
> Like silence, coming after battle roar,
> Now peace comes home and all the storms that shook
> The heart's foundation are no more, no more.
> Now, unafraid, I watch the level length
> Of shadows deepen into darkest night:
> Here in my hands is quietness and strength,
> Here in my hands is gentleness and might.
> Though satellites may whirl in outer space,
> And hearts may faint with fear, this heart of mine
> Is confident. I hold the Book and trace
> God's faithfulness in every single line.
> And though the midnight of the world be nearing,
> I face the dawn - the day of His appearing.

The family blessed of God is the family where the Word of God is considered truly a love letter.

Personal Notes

1 John 4:7-21

Beloved, let us love one another, for love is of God; and everyone who loves is born of God and knows God.
He who does not love does not know God, for God is love. In this the love of God was manifested toward us, that God has sent His only begotten Son into the world, that we might live through Him. In this is love, not that we loved God, but that He loved us and sent His Son to be the propitiation for our sins. Beloved, if God so loved us, we also ought to love one another. No one has seen God at any time. If we love one another, God abides in us, and His love has been perfected in us. By this we know that we abide in Him, and He in us, because He has given us of His Spirit. And we have seen and testify that the Father has sent the Son as Saviour of the world. Whoever confesses that Jesus is the Son of God, God abides in him, and he in God. And we have known and believed the love that God has for us. God is love, and he who abides in love abides in God, and God in him. Love has been perfected among us in this: that we may have boldness in the day of judgment; because as He is, so are we in this world. There is no fear in love; but perfect love casts out fear, because fear involves torment. But he who fears has not been made perfect in love. We love Him because He first loved us. If someone says, "I love God," and hates his brother, he is a liar; for he who does not love his brother whom he has seen, how can he love God whom he has not seen? And this commandment we have from Him: that he who loves God must love his brother also.

The Path of Duty

As the people of Israel stood on the threshold of the Promised Land, God, through the leadership of Moses, instructed the people in their responsibility for assuring themselves of the Lord's continued blessing. They were deeply aware of the consequences of removing themselves from His blessing. They had witnessed an entire generation of men die in the wilderness within the previous forty years because of faithlessness and disobedience. Now they were back to the doorstep of blessing and anxious to trust in the living God.

Moses began instruction by telling the people where a home blessed of God starts: "Here, O Israel: The Lord our God, the Lord is one. Love the Lord your God with all your heart and with all your soul and with all your strength" (Deuteronomy 6:4-5 NIV). Israel's call to love God was focused upon the revelation of Himself as their only true deliverer and provider. He delivered them from Egyptian bondage, He met all their physical needs for survival, and He provided a means for them to have their sins covered through sacrifice. To love God with the whole personality was a natural response, given His personal commitment to them. Love for the Lord was in Moses' day, and still is today, where God's blessings begin.

The apostle John tells us that we love God, because He first loved us and gave himself for us (see I John 4). Calvary was not just a model of love, but a point of substitution: Christ's suffering for man's sin, Christ's death for man's damnation. It is Calvary truth, more than any other truth that stirs hearts to the love for God that so positively affects the home.

Charles Spurgeon spoke of such love: "Love to Christ smooths the path of duty, and wings the feet to travel it: it makes the life of sincere devotion. Love has a clear eye; but it can see only one thing - it is blind to every interest but that of its Lord; love sees things in the light of his glory, and weighs actions on the scales of his honour; love counts royalty but drudgery if it cannot reign for Christ, but it delights in servitude as much as in honour, if it can thereby advance the Master's kingdom; love's end sweetens all its means; love's object lightens all its toil."

There is great blessing to be found in God for every family on earth, and many stand at the threshold. How many will turn back, missing Calvary truth and consequently be in want of love for God.

Personal Notes

Romans 8:26-34

Likewise the Spirit also helps in our weaknesses. For we do not know what we should pray for as we ought, but the Spirit Himself makes intercession for us with groanings which cannot be uttered. Now He who searches the hearts knows what the mind of the Spirit is, because He makes intercession for the saints according to the will of God. And we know that all things work together for good to those who love God, to those who are the called according to His purpose.For whom He foreknew, He also predestined to be conformed to the image of His Son, that He might be the firstborn among many brethren. Moreover whom He predestined, these He also called; whom He called, these He also justified; and whom He justified, these He also glorified.What then shall we say to these things? If God is for us, who can be against us? He who did not spare His own Son, but delivered Him up for us all, how shall He not with Him also freely give us all things? Who shall bring a charge against God's elect? It is God who justifies. Who is he who condemns? It is Christ who died, and furthermore is also risen, who is even at the right hand of God, who also makes intercession for us.

Conformed to Christ

My son and I sat down to plan the careful carving up of a small block of wood that hopefully would resemble a race car to be entered in the AWANA children's club grand-prix. My son came to me with his favourite micro racer and asked if we could use it as a model; all we had to do is remove all the wood in the block that didn't look like the prototype. That thought reminded me of what the Lord's intention within the life of those who have come to know Jesus as Saviour. God, in desiring to "bring many sons to glory" (Hebrews 2:10), is daily moulding His children "to be conformed to the image of His son" (Romans 8:29).

God's process of chipping away all that is in a believer that does not resemble Christ may involve hardship, loss, sorrow or stress. However, for those believers who turn all life's choices over to the Lord there is the wonderful promise that "all things work together for good" (Romans 8:28). In this past year of economic woe, it has been a privilege to witness many of God's children rise above the stressful circumstances which often brought loss, by drawing closer to the Lord in earnest faith to be more made like the Son who suffered for us. In such lives there has been an increased tenderness for the suffering people of the world, there has been a deepening awareness of the terrible circumstances of all who are outside the family of God through unbelief, there has been, by necessity, movement toward a total walk of faith resulting in living evidence of the grace of God. All of this, "being made like Jesus", has turned some sceptical eyes heavenward in search of what these believers have found: "the peace that passes understanding" (Philippians 4:7).

With God accomplishing so much in that process of "chipping away", is it any wonder that James calls the believer to "consider it pure joy whenever you face trials of many kinds" (James 1:2). To each believer who has by faith, welcomed these trials of loss and hardship in joy, God shares this promise: "Blessed is the man who perseveres under, because when he has stood the test, he will receive the victor's crown of life which God has promised those who love him" (James 1:12).

Personal Notes

2 Corinthians 3:1-11

Do we begin again to commend ourselves? Or do we need, as some others, epistles of commendation to you or letters of commendation from you? You are our epistle written in our hearts, known and read by all men; clearly you are an epistle of Christ, ministered by us, written not with ink but by the Spirit of the living God, not on tablets of stone but on tablets of flesh, that is, of the heart. And we have such trust through Christ toward God. Not that we are sufficient of ourselves to think of anything as being from ourselves, but our sufficiency is from God, who also made us sufficient as ministers of the new covenant, not of the letter but of the Spirit; for the letter kills, but the Spirit gives life. But if the ministry of death, written and engraved on stones, was glorious, so that the children of Israel could not look steadily at the face of Moses because of the glory of his countenance, which glory was passing away, how will the ministry of the Spirit not be more glorious? For if the ministry of condemnation had glory, the ministry of righteousness exceeds much more in glory. For even what was made glorious had no glory in this respect, because of the glory that excels. For if what is passing away was glorious, what remains is much more glorious.

Walking Epistles

"How do you read me?" These may be common words to the amateur radio operator, but they are also words every Christian should be asking. Paul, writing to the believers at Corinth, said they were his "epistle ... known and read of all men." He wrote to the church at Thessalonica and said their "faith toward God had gone forth, so that he had no need to say anything." The Bible makes it clear; true believers are to "deny ungodliness and worldly desires and live sensibly, righteously, and godly in this present age." To His children, God commands "Conduct yourselves with wisdom toward outsiders, making the most of the opportunity." This is of utmost importance because, as the saying states, "You are the only Bible the needy world may read."

Every Christian is called upon to be a living epistle, known and read by those around them. Jesus said, "Let your light so shine before men that they may see our good works and glorify your father which is in heaven."

On the other hand, the Epistle of James states: "Faith, if it has no works, is dead, being by itself." To the professing Christian whose life is void of a testimony for God, Paul says "Test yourselves, to see if you are in the faith, examine yourselves. Christ is in you unless indeed you fail the test." We live in a society where less than 6% of the population attend church and where violence, corruption, deceit and injustice are worse than anyone would have imagined even ten years ago. Truly this is a world that desperately needs to "hear" from God. The importance of each believer's testimony is clear. The Lord intended the Christian faith to be READ not DEAD. Christian friend, how is the world reading you?

Personal Notes

Isaiah 42:1-9

"Behold! My Servant whom I uphold, My Elect One in whom My soul delights! I have put My Spirit upon Him; He will bring forth justice to the Gentiles. He will not cry out, nor raise His voice, Nor cause His voice to be heard in the street. A bruised reed He will not break, And smoking flax He will not quench; He will bring forth justice for truth. He will not fail nor be discouraged, Till He has established justice in the earth; And the coastlands shall wait for His law."

Thus says God the LORD, Who created the heavens and stretched them out, Who spread forth the earth and that which comes from it, Who gives breath to the people on it, And spirit to those who walk on it: "I, the LORD, have called You in righteousness, And will hold Your hand; I will keep You and give You as a covenant to the people, As a light to the Gentiles, To open blind eyes, To bring out prisoners from the prison, Those who sit in darkness from the prison house. I am the LORD, that is My name; And My glory I will not give to another, Nor My praise to carved images. Behold, the former things have come to pass, And new things I declare; Before they spring forth I tell you of them."

To Be Served or To Serve – That is the Question!

Captain Bligh was senior officer of the ship called *The Bounty*. The book "Mutiny on the Bounty" reveals Captain Bligh as quite a scoundrel. His leadership as captain inspired hatred and rebellion. However, in the sequel to "Mutiny on the Bounty" called "Men Against the Sea", Mr. Bligh and a few loyal officers were set adrift in a small open launch in the middle of the ocean. Captain Bligh led these 19 men 3600 miles to safety. That was a remarkable accomplishment in a small, unarmed launch. Here Captain Bligh didn't inspire hatred and rebellion; rather, his leadership inspired courage and confidence.

In all mankind's relationships and in every responsibility, great or small, there is potential to either inspire hatred and rebellion, or courage and confidence. The deciding factor is our attitude toward others. In his book called "The Marriage Builder", Dr. Lawrence Crabb suggests that people live out their lives either as manipulators, seeking their own self-interest, or as ministers, seeking to meet the needs of others.

Jesus addressed this very issue when he taught the disciples that their greatest impact in sharing His Gospel would come through following His example of servant leadership. Jesus said: "even the Son of man came not to be served, but to serve, and to give his life a ransom for many." (Mark 10:45). Christ's death on the cross as a substitute for man's sin-guilt was the supreme expression of servanthood.

Servanthood hardly fits today's "I'm worth it" attitude, nevertheless, God's call to His people is just that: "Let no man seek his own, but every man another's [well-being]." (1 Corinthians. 10:24). In order to be free to minister to others in a way that will inspire confidence and courage, our own needs must be first met by the God of "living waters". As individuals come to Christ for His gift of eternal life, trusting in His sacrifice for their sins, they are brought into a special relationship with God: "But as many as received him, to them gave he the power (authority) to become the sons (children) of God, [even] to them that believe on his name" (John 1:12). As God's children walk in obedience and trust before Him, God confirms His care and pleasure within their hearts, satisfying the deepest needs. The result is freedom to minister rather than manipulate.

Are you a Captain Bligh on the "Bounty," viewing all others as your servants, or a Captain Bligh "Against the Sea" viewing yourself as a servant with the task of bringing others to safety - in Christ?

Personal Notes

Matthew 20:20-28

Then the mother of Zebedee's sons came to Him with her sons, kneeling down and asking something from Him. And He said to her, "What do you wish?" She said to Him, "Grant that these two sons of mine may sit, one on Your right hand and the other on the left, in Your kingdom." But Jesus answered and said, "You do not know what you ask. Are you able to drink the cup that I am about to drink, and be baptized with the baptism that I am baptized with?" They said to Him, "We are able." So He said to them, "You will indeed drink My cup, and be baptized with the baptism that I am baptized with; but to sit on My right hand and on My left is not Mine to give, but it is for those for whom it is prepared by My Father." And when the ten heard it, they were greatly displeased with the two brothers. But Jesus called them to Himself and said, "You know that the rulers of the Gentiles lord it over them, and those who are great exercise authority over them. "Yet it shall not be so among you; but whoever desires to become great among you, let him be your servant. "And whoever desires to be first among you, let him be your slave— "just as the Son of Man did not come to be served, but to serve, and to give His life a ransom for many."

Counting the Cost

Someone once told me that if you are planning to renovate a house, you calculate the cost as accurately as possible, then double it and you will be close to actual costs. Whether this is true or not, I do not know; however, it serves to reinforce the need to count the cost before committing.

In this money-conscious, cut-back and make-do world our society is learning that there are some things worth paying for, such as health care and education. Accepting the cost may hurt, but the alternatives are far more dangerous.

It was to this very kind of a situation that Christ addressed these remarks regarding discipleship: "And anyone who does not carry his cross and follow me cannot be my disciple. Suppose one of you wants to build a tower. Will he not first sit down and estimate the cost to see if he has enough money to complete it? For if he lays the foundation and is not able to finish it, everyone who sees it will ridicule him, saying, `This fellow began to build and was not able to finish" (Luke 14:27-30 NIV).

Christ was not seeking to discourage those who put their trust in him, but was expressing the real cost of loving God. Although salvation is free, ("For the wages of sin is death; but the gift of God is eternal life through Jesus Christ our Lord" Romans 6:23), those who receive by faith this gift of life are brought into a new relationship with God that alienates the believer from the unbelieving world, ("Now to you who believe, this stone (Christ) is precious. But to those who do not believe, "The stone the builders rejected has become the capstone," and, "A stone that causes men to stumble and a rock that makes them fall." They stumble because they disobey the message" 1 Peter 2 NIV).

Jesus Christ, God's own Son, has provided a means for man to be restored to fellowship with Holy God. In the text of Luke 14, Jesus is demonstrating that although the result (cost) of new life in Christ may indeed alienate the believer from even family, the life without Christ's gift is far worse than any hardship which the gift of life could bring. This anonymous poem makes the point:

"I counted all my dollars while God counted crosses; I counted gains while he counted losses; I counted my worth by the things gained in store, But He sized me up by the scars that I bore. I coveted honours and sought for degrees; He wept as He counted the hours on my knees. I never knew till one day by a grave, How vain are the things that we spend life to save. I did not know till a friend went above - That richest is he who is rich in God's love."

The old hymn asks the important question: "Have you counted the cost, if your soul should be lost, though you gain the whole world for your own... have you counted the cost?"

Personal Notes

Hebrews 11:1-11

Now faith is the substance of things hoped for, the evidence of things not seen. For by it the elders obtained a good testimony. By faith we understand that the worlds were framed by the word of God, so that the things which are seen were not made of things which are visible. By faith Abel offered to God a more excellent sacrifice than Cain, through which he obtained witness that he was righteous, God testifying of his gifts; and through it he being dead still speaks. By faith Enoch was taken away so that he did not see death, "and was not found, because God had taken him"; for before he was taken he had this testimony, that he pleased God. But without faith it is impossible to please Him, for he who comes to God must believe that He is, and that He is a rewarder of those who diligently seek Him. By faith Noah, being divinely warned of things not yet seen, moved with godly fear, prepared an ark for the saving of his household, by which he condemned the world and became heir of the righteousness which is according to faith. By faith Abraham obeyed when he was called to go out to the place which he would receive as an inheritance. And he went out, not knowing where he was going. By faith he dwelt in the land of promise as in a foreign country, dwelling in tents with Isaac and Jacob, the heirs with him of the same promise; for he waited for the city which has foundations, whose builder and maker is God. By faith Sarah herself also received strength to conceive seed, and she bore a child when she was past the age, because she judged Him faithful who had promised.

By Faith...

In my school days the music teacher would bring the class into harmony with the pitch pipe. That tiny instrument in the hands of the right person could start an entire class of rowdy children off to a harmonious expression of song. In a similar way the operating principle of the gospel ("The just shall live by faith" Romans 1:17), plays the lead in the believer's life, not just as a point of entrance to that distinguished plateau, but as the deliberate path of life.

Faith is the door to the often denied but very real spiritual world of eternal life: "For by grace are ye saved through faith; and that not of yourselves: [it is] the gift of God" (Ephesians 2:8). Faith is the note by which all the Christian's life-songs should begin: "For we walk by faith, not by sight" 2 Corinthians 5:7. Faith, says scripture is "the substance (title deed) of things hoped for, the evidence (proof) of things not seen." (Hebrews 11:1).

This deliberate path that the believer is called to follow is illustrated in this summary of Moses' life: "By faith Moses... refused to be called the son of Pharaoh's daughter; Choosing rather to suffer affliction with the people of God, than to enjoy the pleasures of sin for a season; Esteeming the reproach of Christ greater riches than the treasures in Egypt: for he had respect unto the recompense of the reward. By faith he forsook Egypt, not fearing the wrath of the king: for he endured, as seeing him who is invisible. Through faith he kept the passover, and the sprinkling of blood," (Hebrews 11)

Notice how deliberate the steps of the path of faith are: Step One - Making A Choice (turning from sin to God), Step Two - Accepting The Cost (turning from temporary wealth to eternal reward), Step Three - Embracing A Commitment (overcoming fear and following God's path), Step Four - Pursuing Continuance (staying obedient and maintaining a vital relationship with God). This is not just a short excursion, but a life-long pursuit.

One final point is important to consider regarding this deliberate path of faith. It is the fruit of clear and definite knowledge, the knowledge of Jesus Christ, "In whom are hid all the treasures of wisdom and knowledge." (Colossians 2:3). Therefore, this deliberate path of faith is not a tour in blindness or ignorance, on the contrary, it is nothing less than wisdom and prudence; it dictates, distinguishes, teaches, and is science and knowledge.

For any life to be in tune with God, that life must be first reconciled to God by faith in Christ, then continue to live by faith in the promises and priorities that the Lord reveals in His Holy Word, the Bible. This is living by faith! Are you tuned to God's song of living?

Personal Notes

John 15:1-10

"I am the true vine, and My Father is the vinedresser. "Every branch in Me that does not bear fruit He takes away; and every branch that bears fruit He prunes, that it may bear more fruit. "You are already clean because of the word which I have spoken to you. "Abide in Me, and I in you. As the branch cannot bear fruit of itself, unless it abides in the vine, neither can you, unless you abide in Me. "I am the vine, you are the branches. He who abides in Me, and I in him, bears much fruit; for without Me you can do nothing. "If anyone does not abide in Me, he is cast out as a branch and is withered; and they gather them and throw them into the fire, and they are burned. "If you abide in Me, and My words abide in you, you will ask what you desire, and it shall be done for you. "By this My Father is glorified, that you bear much fruit; so you will be My disciples. "As the Father loved Me, I also have loved you; abide in My love. "If you keep My commandments, you will abide in My love, just as I have kept My Father's commandments and abide in His love.

Raining Flowers

As these cold winter days drag causing "blue" days for some, Robert Loveman's poem comes to mind: "It isn't raining rain to me, it's raining daffodils! In every dimpling drop I see - Wild flowers on the hills! A cloud of grey engulfs the day - and overwhelms the town; It isn't raining rain to me it's raining roses down!"

I'm sure that every reader desires to have the kind of joy that can turn grey days into daffodils and that can see the silver lining of every clouded situation. For most, however, it is simple wishful thinking. Yet, for those who know the Lord Jesus as personal Saviour, this joy can be a reality. Jesus said: "These things have I spoken unto you, that my joy might remain in you, and [that] your joy might be full." (John 15:11)

The pathway to this joy is made clear in the text by the repetition of the phrase "abide in me" (referred to nine times in verses 4 through 10). To 'abide in Christ' means to keep up a habit of constant close communion with Him, to be always leaning on Him, resting on Him, pouring out our hearts to Him, and using Him as our Fountain of life and strength, as our chief Companion and best Friend.

"Abiding", in this passage, is to have His Word abiding in us (verse 7), to keep His sayings and precepts continually before our minds and to make the guide of our actions and the rule of our life (verse 10). "Abiding" is to let the love of God rule our relationships and conduct (verse 12).

Such "abiding in Christ" brings the joy of answered prayer (verse 7), the joy of assured participation in the work of God (verse 8 - "bearing fruit"), and the joy of sensing the love of God. This last joy is alone a deep and satisfying privilege. The feeling of God the Father toward the Son is too high a thing for man to enter. Yet such is the love of the Son toward those who believe in Him, a vast, wide, deep, immeasurable love that passes knowledge and can only be sensed in part by man and turns night into day, wipes tears from the eyes and soothes the hurting heart.

Thoro Harris captured the wonder of this "joy of abiding" in the words to his song: "Who can cheer the heart like Jesus, by His presence all divine? True and tender, pure and precious, O how blest to call Him mine! All that thrills my soul is Jesus, He is more than life to me; And the fairest of ten thousand, In my blessed Lord I see."

Even the winter "blues" can become a season of sunshine when the joy of the Lord is discovered. You find it when "abiding in Him."

Personal Notes

Hebrews 6:9-18

But, beloved, we are confident of better things concerning you, yes, things that accompany salvation, though we speak in this manner. For God is not unjust to forget your work and labour of love which you have shown toward His name, in that you have ministered to the saints, and do minister. And we desire that each one of you show the same diligence to the full assurance of hope until the end, that you do not become sluggish, but imitate those who through faith and patience inherit the promises. For when God made a promise to Abraham, because He could swear by no one greater, He swore by Himself, saying, "Surely blessing I will bless you, and multiplying I will multiply you." And so, after he had patiently endured, he obtained the promise. For men indeed swear by the greater, and an oath for confirmation is for them an end of all dispute. Thus God, determining to show more abundantly to the heirs of promise the immutability of His counsel, confirmed it by an oath, that by two immutable things, in which it is impossible for God to lie, we might have strong consolation, who have fled for refuge to lay hold of the hope set before us.

God's Own Honour Roll

There was an article in the *Readers Digest* a few years ago about a public school principal in a tough neighbourhood of Edmonton who turned the attitude of the students completely around. His method was not one of rebuke, but one of reward. He invented "honour rolls" for just about every imaginable achievement possible. As a result, practically every child had opportunity to be recognized for some achievement.

It would seem that once the students saw the principal as a passionate person as well as an authority figure, he was able to gain their confidence. In so doing he won the respect of the neighbourhood and his positive influence extended far beyond the school ground.

Our world needs to see the Lord God in that same way; not only as supreme in authority but as deep in passion. To do so the Lord has established His own "honour roll". The list begins in Hebrews 11 where God recognizes Abel, Enoch, Noah, Abraham and Sarah, Isaac, Jacob, Joseph, Moses, and many others. The criteria for making the honour roll is faith, and the Lord makes it clear that the list is still being added to: "But without faith [it is] impossible to please [him]:

for he that cometh to God must believe that he is, and [that] he is a rewarder of them that diligently seek him." (Hebrews 11:6).

Let all those who, by faith, have come to know Christ as personal Saviour and who by faith have turned their attention to the will of God rather than self-interest, know that He rewards. For all who have faced rebuke, ridicule, and even rejection because of the choice to "love the Lord your God with all your heart and with all your soul and with all your mind" (Matthew 22:37), God has an honour roll that will last through eternity. Be reminded of these closing words of scripture: "And, behold, I come quickly; and my reward [is] with me, to give every man according as his work shall be." (Revelation 22:12)

The Lord calls each believer to take up his or her cross daily (Luke 9:23). For some this means heartache, for others, ceaseless care, and still others, great burden. Yet in all this, God ensures each Christian of this promise: "God is not unjust; he will not forget your work and the love you have shown him as you have helped his people and continue to help them." (Hebrews 6:10 NIV). For this reason the attitude of the believer should always be as Paul's: "For our light and momentary troubles are achieving for us an eternal glory that far outweighs them all. So we fix our eyes not on what is seen, but on what is unseen. For what is seen is temporary, but what is unseen is eternal. (2 Corinthians 4:17-18 NIV).

With God's honour list in view, let every committed Christian determine not to grow weary in well-doing!

Personal Notes

Titus 3:1-8

Remind them to be subject to rulers and authorities, to obey, to be ready for every good work, to speak evil of no one, to be peaceable, gentle, showing all humility to all men. For we ourselves were also once foolish, disobedient, deceived, serving various lusts and pleasures, living in malice and envy, hateful and hating one another. But when the kindness and the love of God our Saviour toward man appeared, not by works of righteousness which we have done, but according to His mercy He saved us, through the washing of regeneration and renewing of the Holy Spirit, whom He poured out on us abundantly through Jesus Christ our Saviour, that having been justified by His grace we should become heirs according to the hope of eternal life. This is a faithful saying, and these things I want you to affirm constantly, that those who have believed in God should be careful to maintain good works. These things are good and profitable to men.

Gracious Grace

Every licensed driver dreads that red flashing light in the rear view mirror that announces to the world our wrong doing. Yet, as much as the experience is unpleasant, honesty forces an admittance of guilt within ourselves. That's why, on those unique occasions after a short rebuke from the officer, the following words are music to our ears: "I'm going to be gracious this time!" The mere mention of grace allows hope to rise that we are not going to get the stiff fine that we deserve.

Getting something better than deserved is as good a definition of grace as any. That's exactly what Salvation from God is all about. Paul, writing to the Ephesians stated: "For by grace are ye saved through faith; and that not of yourselves: [it is] the gift of God" (Ephesians 2:8) This Salvation, which delivers man from a condemned condition because of sin (see Romans 3:23) to an acquitted position before God (see Romans 8:1) is entirely undeserved! So much so that the first step to finding it is an admission before God of guilt, and sorrow of heart for the offence that sin is to a Holy God.

This first step in reality is a description of repentance -the change of mind about man's own worthiness that calls for the necessity of faith in the complete substitution of Christ as our sin bearer. Although often glossed over in our day of self-satisfaction, repentance is a fundamental part of the path to forgiveness from God. Repentance has been described as the flip side of the coin of faith, without it there is no salvation!

In the text cited above, faith reaches out to accept Christ's work on the cross that offers eternal life (the gift of God), repentance turns from man's fruitless self-effort to gain approval ("saved - not of ourselves") which ends in eternal death: "Not by works of righteousness which we have done, but according to his mercy he saved us," (Titus 3:5).

Understanding and accepting our own guilt brings the hope of God's message of grace - getting what we do not deserve. This is what the Lord meant when he said: "Blessed are the poor in spirit, for theirs is the kingdom of heaven." (Matthew 5:3 NIV). He was referring to all who acknowledge their own spiritual poverty and therefore hear the message of grace.

Here then is God's flashing red light: "Cursed is the one who trusts in man, who depends on flesh for his strength and whose heart turns away from the LORD." (Jeremiah 17:5), and here are God's words of music to man's ears: "For God so loved the world that he gave his one and only Son, that whoever believes in him shall not perish but have eternal life. (John 3:16 NIV) ...I tell you the truth, whoever hears my word and believes him who sent me has eternal life and will not be condemned; he has crossed over from death to life" (John 5:24 NIV).

Personal Notes

81

Romans 3:20-26

Therefore by the deeds of the law no flesh will be justified in His sight, for by the law is the knowledge of sin. But now the righteousness of God apart from the law is revealed, being witnessed by the Law and the Prophets, even the righteousness of God, through faith in Jesus Christ, to all and on all who believe. For there is no difference; for all have sinned and fall short of the glory of God, being justified freely by His grace through the redemption that is in Christ Jesus, whom God set forth as a propitiation by His blood, through faith, to demonstrate His righteousness, because in His forbearance God had passed over the sins that were previously committed, to demonstrate at the present time His righteousness, that He might be just and the justifier of the one who has faith in Jesus.

The Lifted Burden

John Bunyan, in his story *Pilgrim's Progress*, graphically portrayed the point of salvation of young Christian: "Up this way, therefore, did burdened Christian run, but not without great difficulty, because of the load on his back. He ran thus till he came at a place somewhat ascending, and upon that place stood a cross and a little below, in the bottom, a sepulchre. So I saw in my dream, that just as Christian came up with the cross, his burden loosed from off his shoulder, and fell from off his back, and began to tumble, and so continued to do until it came to the mouth of the sepulchre, where if fell in, and I saw it no more. Then was Christian glad and lightsome, and said with a merry heart, "He hath given me rest by His sorrow and life by His death."

In the footnotes, Bunyan explains the scripture truth of salvation: "Christian had faith; he believed that there was redemption in the blood of Christ, even forgiveness of sins, before he came up to the cross, but now he finds and feels the comfort of it: He has now the joy of faith, the guilt of sins is taken off his conscience, and he is filled with joy and peace in believing."

Some would dismiss Bunyan as a radical puritan; nevertheless, he was faithful, even in prison, to the truth of the gospel message. Unlike many clergy today, Bunyan would not compromise the truth of personal sin and necessity of repentance: "For all have sinned, and come short of the glory of God" (Romans 3:23), "Repent ye therefore, and be converted, that your sins may be blotted out, when times of refreshing shall come from the Lord" (Acts 3:19). Bunyan would not soften the judgment of Holy God, nor think it distasteful to speak of the cleansing power of the blood of Christ: "And as it is appointed unto men once to die, but after this the judgment" (Hebrews 9:27), "In whom we have redemption through his blood, the forgiveness of sins, according to the riches of his grace" (Ephesians 1:7).

The burden on Christian's back was the weight of sin he felt before a Holy God. Only those who acknowledge their sin and, with the remorse of its burden, turn to Christ in faith for cleansing through His blood, will ever find the peace of salvation. Repentance and trust are, in essence, two aspects of the same decision of faith. Repentance is the heart's turning away from any effort of self by the acceptance of personal spiritual poverty; it is the sorrow of sin and admission of helplessness. Trust is the heart's turning to Christ in belief of His sacrifice on the cross as personal substitute for sin's judgement of death, in belief of His resurrection as victory over death and giver of eternal life.

The great truth of salvation is still sung today: "Burdens are lifted at Calvary, Jesus is very near". Where is your burden?

Personal Notes

Ephesians 3:13-21

Therefore I ask that you do not lose heart at my tribulations for you, which is your glory. For this reason I bow my knees to the Father of our Lord Jesus Christ, from whom the whole family in heaven and earth is named, that He would grant you, according to the riches of His glory, to be strengthened with might through His Spirit in the inner man, that Christ may dwell in your hearts through faith; that you, being rooted and grounded in love, may be able to comprehend with all the saints what is the width and length and depth and height— to know the love of Christ which passes knowledge; that you may be filled with all the fullness of God. Now to Him who is able to do exceedingly abundantly above all that we ask or think, according to the power that works in us, to Him be glory in the church by Christ Jesus to all generations, forever and ever. Amen.

Rooted in God's Love

As Valentine's Day approaches and special gifts are secured for those that are our closest loved ones, let us also be mindful of the love that is perpetually extended to us. I speak of the love of God: "For God so loved the world, that he gave his only begotten Son" (John 3:16).

Paul shares the wonder of this love: "that you, being rooted and grounded in love, May be able to comprehend with all saints what [is] the breadth, and length, and depth, and height; And to know the love of Christ, which passes knowledge, that ye might be filled with all the fullness of God." (Ephesians 3). Paul reminded the Romans that this love was unconquerable: "For I am persuaded, that neither death, nor life, nor angels, nor principalities, nor powers, nor things present, nor things to come, Nor height, nor depth, nor any other creature, shall be able to separate us from the love of God, which is in Christ Jesus our Lord." (Romans 8)

This love is the theme of Amy Carmichael booklet "If", in which she reflects upon this love of God: "There are times when something comes into our lives which is charged with love in such a way that it seems to open the Eternal to us for a moment, or at least some of the Eternal Things, and the greatest of these is love.

It may be a small and intimate touch upon us or our affairs, light as the touch of the dawn-wind on the leaves of the tree, something not to be captured and told to another in words. But we know that it is our Lord. And then perhaps the room where we are, with its furniture and books and flowers, seems less "present" than His Presence, and the heart is drawn into that sweetness of which the old hymn sings: The love of Jesus what it is, None but His loved ones know."

Do you want to experience a real love that never fails, never fades, never loses interest, never gets side tracked, and never ever disowns? Then come to the Saviour, put your life in his hands and discover what Eugene Clark discovered:

"Jesus' love will never fail me; He's a faithful friend and guide,
Leading me through joy and sorrow, Constantly He's by my side.
Jesus' love will never fail me. "Trust me," I can hear Him say,
"I will never, ever leave you, Nor forsake you, come what may."
Jesus' love will never fail me; His own life He freely gave,
Proving just how much He loved me, When He died my soul to save.
Jesus' love will never fail me; Faith and trust are on the throne;
Doubt and fear no longer haunt me, As I face things yet unknown.
Life will bring both joy and sorrow, On Jesus' love I can rely;
All things for my good are working, There's no need to question why."

Personal Notes

1 John 3:14-23

We know that we have passed from death to life, because we love the brethren. He who does not love his brother abides in death. Whoever hates his brother is a murderer, and you know that no murderer has eternal life abiding in him. By this we know love, because He laid down His life for us. And we also ought to lay down our lives for the brethren. But whoever has this world's goods, and sees his brother in need, and shuts up his heart from him, how does the love of God abide in him? My little children, let us not love in word or in tongue, but in deed and in truth. And by this we know that we are of the truth, and shall assure our hearts before Him. For if our heart condemns us, God is greater than our heart, and knows all things. Beloved, if our heart does not condemn us, we have confidence toward God. And whatever we ask we receive from Him, because we keep His commandments and do those things that are pleasing in His sight. And this is His commandment: that we should believe on the name of His Son Jesus Christ and love one another, as He gave us commandment.

Active Love

Once again the Valentine season brings thoughts of love and romance. Often this love is expressed by cards and gifts during a short season, yet taken for granted most of the year. Christian love should have a more direct bearing on everyday life. In the Russian novel, *The Brothers Karamazov*, a woman has her problems with faith. "What if I've been believing all my life, and when I come to die there is nothing but burdocks growing over my grave? ... How can I prove it? How can I convince myself?" The reply is: "By the experience of active love. Insofar as you advance in active love, you will grow surer of the reality of God and of the immortality of the soul."

It is an active love that God calls the believer to bring to the world. A love modeled after God himself who "... demonstrated His own love toward us in that while we were yet sinners, Christ died for us" (Romans 5:8).

Active love was evident in this exert from *Through the Valley of the Kwai* by Ernest Gordon. "We found ourselves on the same track with several carloads of Japanese wounded after we were freed from the Kwai prison camp. These unfortunates were on their own without medical care. No longer fit for action in Burma, they had been packed into railway cars which were being returned to Bangkok.

They were in a shocking state. I have never seen men filthier. Uniforms were encrusted with mud, blood, and excrement. Their wounds, sorely inflamed and full of pus, crawled with maggots. The maggots, however, in eating the putrefying flesh, probably prevented gangrene. It was apparent why the Japanese were so cruel to their prisoners. If they didn't care for their own, why should they care for us?

The wounded looked at us forlornly as they sat with their heads resting against the carriages, waiting for death. They had been discarded as expendable, the refuse of war. These were the enemy. They were more cowed and defeated than we had ever been.

Without a word most of the officers in my section unbuckled their packs, took out part of their ration and a rag or two, and, with water canteens in their hands, went over to the Japanese train. Our guards tried to prevent us, bawling, "No goodka! No goodka!" But we ignored them and knelt down by the enemy to give water and food, to clean and bind up their wounds.

Grateful cries of "Aragatto!" ("Thank you") followed us when we left--. I regarded my comrades with wonder. Eighteen months ago they would have joined readily in the destruction of our captors had they fallen into their hands. Now these same officers were dressing the enemy's wounds.

We had experienced a moment of grace, there in those bloodstained railway cars. God had broken through the barriers of our prejudice and had given us the will to obey His command, "Thou shalt love..." Christian friend, how active is your love?

Personal Notes

Luke 6:27-36

"But I say to you who hear: Love your enemies, do good to those who hate you, "bless those who curse you, and pray for those who spitefully use you. "To him who strikes you on the one cheek, offer the other also. And from him who takes away your cloak, do not withhold your tunic either. "Give to everyone who asks of you. And from him who takes away your goods do not ask them back. "And just as you want men to do to you, you also do to them likewise. "But if you love those who love you, what credit is that to you? For even sinners love those who love them. "And if you do good to those who do good to you, what credit is that to you? For even sinners do the same. "And if you lend to those from whom you hope to receive back, what credit is that to you? For even sinners lend to sinners to receive as much back. "But love your enemies, do good, and lend, hoping for nothing in return; and your reward will be great, and you will be sons of the Most High. For He is kind to the unthankful and evil. "Therefore be merciful, just as your Father also is merciful.

Christian Love

A popular song years ago stated "What the world needs now is love, sweet love, it's the only thing that there is just too little of." Although I wouldn't agree that it's the only thing there is too little of, I would agree that love is desperately lacking. This is especially apparent among Christians, considering that Christ spoke so importantly of it. "Thou shalt love the Lord thy God with all thy heart, and with all thy soul, and with all thy strength, and with all thy mind; and thy neighbour as thyself." (Luke 10:27). "But I say unto you which hear, Love your enemies, do good to them which hate you" (Luke 6:27).

Perhaps it's time to remind ourselves as believers and followers of Christ that ordinary words were not enough to describe the affection the first Christians felt for one another. So they took an old word 'agape' that had fallen into disuse. They dusted it off and infused it with new meaning. The apostle Paul was led to write these great truths about that love: "Love suffers long and is kind; love does not envy; love does not parade itself, is not puffed up; does not behave rudely, does not seek its own, is not provoked, thinks no evil; does not rejoice in iniquity, but rejoices in the truth; bears all things, believes all things, hopes all things, endures all things. Love never fails." (1 Corinthians 13).

Others as well have seen the uniqueness of Christian love. "Love is the one ingredient of which our world never tires and of which there is never an abundance. It is needed in the marketplace and in the mansions. It is needed in the ghettos and in the governments. It is needed in homes, in hospitals, and in individual hearts. The world will never outgrow its need for love. " (C. Neil Strait).

Love is the one treasure that multiplies by division. It is the one gift that grows bigger the more you take from it. It is the one business in which it pays to be an absolute spendthrift. You can give it away, throw it away, empty your pockets, shake the basket, turn the glass upside down, and tomorrow you will have more than ever.

"Nothing is sweeter than love, nothing stronger, nothing higher, nothing wider, nothing more pleasant, nothing fuller or better in heaven or on earth.... A lover flies, runs, rejoices.... Love often knows no limits but is fervent beyond measure. Love feels no burden, thinks nothing of labors, attempts what is above its strength, pleads no excuse of impossibility.... Though wearied, it is not tired; though pressed, it is not straitened; though alarmed, it is not confounded; but as a lively flame and burning torch, it forces its way upwards and passes securely through all." (Thomas À Kempis).

The joy of the Christian experience is that God Himself produces this love in a life: "The fruit of the Spirit is love..." (Gal. 5). Christian friend, how genuine is your love?

Personal Notes

John 10:11-18

"I am the good shepherd. The good shepherd gives His life for the sheep. "But a hireling, he who is not the shepherd, one who does not own the sheep, sees the wolf coming and leaves the sheep and flees; and the wolf catches the sheep and scatters them. "The hireling flees because he is a hireling and does not care about the sheep. "I am the good shepherd; and I know My sheep, and am known by My own. "As the Father knows Me, even so I know the Father; and I lay down My life for the sheep. "And other sheep I have which are not of this fold; them also I must bring, and they will hear My voice; and there will be one flock and one shepherd. "Therefore My Father loves Me, because I lay down My life that I may take it again. "No one takes it from Me, but I lay it down of Myself. I have power to lay it down, and I have power to take it again. This command I have received from My Father."

Valentine from a Shepherd

Raymond Aaron, in *Chicken Soup for the Soul*, expresses his sorrow from separation. In despair his eleven year old daughter gave him his "most sacred treasure." She gave him a hand-made heart and this Valentine's poem: "For my Dad, Here is a heart for you to keep, for the big leap you're trying to take. Have fun on your journey. It might be blurry. But when you get there, learn to care. Happy Valentine's Day. Love, Your Daughter."

Like Raymond, many people experience times when it seems no one really cares. However, not all have a daughter to bring a ray of sunshine. There is one who does care, however. Despite what circumstances of despair, Jesus, God's risen Son knows and cares for each person.

The disciples experienced this care of Jesus. To them and to all who call upon Him, He is the Good Shepherd: "I am the good shepherd. The good shepherd lays down his life for the sheep... I know my sheep and my sheep know me-- just as the Father knows me and I know the Father... The reason my Father loves me is that I lay down my life-- only to take it up again... My sheep listen to my voice; I know them, and they follow me. I give them eternal life, and they shall never perish; no-one can snatch them out of my hand" (John 10:11, 14-15, 27-29 NIV).

Here Scripture affirms that the Good Shepherd owns the sheep. The emphasis is not on authority as a master to a slave, but on responsibility as a father to a child. The Lord brings the believer into His own family as a loving Father. Here also the text affirms that the Good Shepherd knows the sheep. As a friend who knows all about us and loves us anyway, so Jesus knows our weaknesses. Yet as with Paul, He whispers "My Grace is sufficient for you" (2 Corinthians 12:9).

In the text, it is evident that the Good Shepherd protects the sheep. Although Christians are often in the midst of very ungodly people and circumstances, like sheep in the midst of wolves, Christ keeps vigil over those who put their trust in Him, completing His perfect will. Yet, whatever His Will is, the very hand that holds the universe together is the same hand that keeps believers for through eternity.

The Good Shepherd leads the sheep. As David discovered: "The LORD is my shepherd; I shall not (be in) want. He makes me to lie down in green pastures: he leads me beside the still waters" (Psalms 23). As Charles Weigle's hymn states: "No one ever cared for me like Jesus, there's no other friend so kind as He."

The Good Shepherd sends this message of love to all mankind: "Verily, verily, I say unto you, I am the door of the sheepfold... by me if any man enter in, he shall be saved, and shall go in and out, and find pasture" (John 10:9). Will you enter His fold?

Personal Notes

Romans 8:31-39

What then shall we say to these things? If God is for us, who can be against us? He who did not spare His own Son, but delivered Him up for us all, how shall He not with Him also freely give us all things? Who shall bring a charge against God's elect? It is God who justifies. Who is he who condemns? It is Christ who died, and furthermore is also risen, who is even at the right hand of God, who also makes intercession for us. Who shall separate us from the love of Christ? Shall tribulation, or distress, or persecution, or famine, or nakedness, or peril, or sword? As it is written: "For Your sake we are killed all day long; We are accounted as sheep for the slaughter." Yet in all these things we are more than conquerors through Him who loved us. For I am persuaded that neither death nor life, nor angels nor principalities nor powers, nor things present nor things to come, nor height nor depth, nor any other created thing, shall be able to separate us from the love of God which is in Christ Jesus our Lord.

Valentine Love

Edith Brock, quoted from *Family Helps* pamphlet suggests the origin of Valentines: "According to legend, the valentine takes its name from a young Christian who once lived in ancient Rome. Like so many of the early Christians, Valentine had been imprisoned because of his faith. Often and longingly he thought of his loved ones, and wanted to assure them of his well-being and his love.

Beyond his cell window grew a cluster of violets. He picked some heart-shaped leaves and pieced them to spell the words, "Remember your Valentine" then sent them off by a friendly dove. On the next day and the next, he sent more messages that simply said, "I love you."

Thus did "the Valentine" have its beginning. On Valentine's Day, people of all ages remember those they love by sending Valentine wishes. In similar fashion, God loves us and sends us gifts to show His affection, not once a year, but every day: "Every good gift and every perfect gift is from above, and cometh down from the Father of lights, with whom is no variableness, neither shadow of turning." (James 1:17). God sends us many blessings: love, joy, peace, health, seasons of sunshine, showers of rain. Best of all, He sent heaven's fairest jewel to earth to become our Saviour. "For God so loved the world, that he gave his only begotten Son, that whosoever believeth in him should not perish, but have everlasting life." (John 3:16) "For Christ also hath once suffered for sins, the just for the unjust, that he might bring us to God, being put to death in the flesh, but made alive by the Spirit" (1 Peter 3:18). In a world so void of true love, it is refreshing to know that God's love is sacrificial, unconditional and eternal. To first see that love expressed in His Son dying in our place stirs the heart in response to trust in Him.

On this Valentine Day, may I urge each reader to take a quiet moment and reflect upon the love of God. He sacrificed His Son on a cruel cross to bear the sins of the world. Is it inappropriate to respond to God's great love by giving Him a valentine, our grateful heart, to show Him that He has not loved in vain? Christina Rossetti penned this chorus to express that very thought: "What can I give Him, poor as I am? If I were a shepherd I would give him a lamb; If I were a wiseman I would do my part; Yet what can I give Him? I can give Him my heart."

Personal Notes

93

Philemon 1:10-19

I appeal to you for my son Onesimus, whom I have begotten while in my chains, who once was unprofitable to you, but now is profitable to you and to me. I am sending him back. You therefore receive him, that is, my own heart, whom I wished to keep with me, that on your behalf he might minister to me in my chains for the gospel. But without your consent I wanted to do nothing, that your good deed might not be by compulsion, as it were, but voluntary. For perhaps he departed for a while for this purpose, that you might receive him forever, no longer as a slave but more than a slave—a beloved brother, especially to me but how much more to you, both in the flesh and in the Lord. If then you count me as a partner, receive him as you would me. But if he has wronged you or owes anything, put that on my account. I, Paul, am writing with my own hand. I will repay—not to mention to you that you owe me even your own self besides.

Settled Accounts

Onesimus was a troubled man! Although he had come to understand the forgiveness of God found though faith in the Lord Jesus Christ, he felt a sense of obligation to his former master. While a slave in the house of Philemon, Onesimus took advantage of the trust invested in him by the family; he stole from Philemon, then ran away. Either of these crimes was punishable by death at the whim of a slave owner.

During his wayward trails, Onesimus came under the ministry of the apostle Paul, who shared the good news of forgiveness and eternal life in Christ. The message was simple enough for a child to understand: "That if you confess with your mouth, "Jesus is Lord," and believe in your heart that God raised him from the dead, you will be saved. For it is with your heart that you believe and are justified, and it is with your mouth that you confess and are saved." (Romans 10 NIV)

Having found new life in Christ, Onesimus knew he had to make amends to those he wronged. But how could he repay? He had no money (like the prodigal son, he undoubtedly spent what he had taken to have a "good time")! What could he offer to undo the wrong he had done? He took his problem to Paul and discovered the true meaning of God's own care.

As it turned out, Paul knew master Philemon well, as a fellow believer and as a committed Christian, even having church meetings in his home. Paul, by the leading of the Spirit of God, wrote a letter on Onesimus' behalf. In his appeal to Philemon to accept back Onesimus, not as a slave, but as a brother in the Lord, Paul made this great statement: "So if you consider me a partner, welcome him as you would welcome me. If he has done you any wrong or owes you anything, charge it to me." (Philemon 1 NIV).

In making this statement "if any debt - put it on my account", Paul captures the essence of what Jesus did for mankind while on the cross. What Paul was willing to do for Onesimus, Jesus has done for all - paid the price of sins debt!. Like Onesimus, all mankind stands "spiritually bankrupt", hopeless to pay the debt of sin. While Christ hung on the cross, He cried "it is finished". The word he spoke meant "the debt is paid!" He spoke of the our debt of sin. Here is the beauty of salvation: even as Philemon was asked to receive Onesimus as "Paul himself", so God the Father receives those who put their trust in Christ, as "His own Son": "Yet to all who received him, to those who believed in his name, he gave the right to become children of God" (John 1:12 NIV).

Have you caught the message of Paul's letter to Philemon? Salvation is Jesus saying "if any wrong - put it on my account!" Will you trust in Him today?

Personal Notes

95

Lamentations 3:14-29

I have become the ridicule of all my people—Their taunting song all the day. He has filled me with bitterness, He has made me drink wormwood. He has also broken my teeth with gravel, and covered me with ashes. You have moved my soul far from peace; I have forgotten prosperity. And I said, "My strength and my hope Have perished from the LORD." Remember my affliction and roaming, The wormwood and the gall. My soul still remembers and sinks within me. This I recall to my mind; therefore, I have hope. Through the LORD'S mercies we are not consumed, because His compassions fail not. They are new every morning; Great is Your faithfulness. "The LORD is my portion," says my soul, "Therefore I hope in Him!" The LORD is good to those who wait for Him, To the soul who seeks Him. It is good that one should hope and wait quietly for the salvation of the LORD. It is good for a man to bear the yoke in his youth. Let him sit alone and keep silent, because God has laid it on him; Let him put his mouth in the dust—There may yet be hope.

The Path from Despair

Jeremiah was in despair. As the prophet of God, he had faithfully delivered the Lord's message of doom because of disobedience. Because that doom spelled the fall of Jerusalem, Jeremiah was branded a traitor, imprisoned, and placed in a deep pit: "So they took Jeremiah and put him into the cistern of Malchijah, the king's son, which was in the courtyard of the guard. They lowered Jeremiah by ropes into the cistern; it had no water in it, only mud, and Jeremiah sank down into the mud." (Jeremiah 38:6 NIV).

Where do you go when you're as low as you can get? Jeremiah chose to cling with faith to the God that had promised "with his own eyes he would see Jerusalem fall!" The prophet's later writing expresses his complete trust and dependence upon God: "Because of the LORD's great love we are not consumed, for his compassions never fail. They are new every morning; great is your faithfulness. I say to myself, "The LORD is my portion; therefore I will wait for him." (Lamentations 3:22-24 NIV).

In the midst of crisis, stress, and yes - even being as low as we can go, God is an ever present help in trouble. His help comes through hearing His Word and trusting in His promises. This is not wishful thinking, nor the power of positive thinking, this is faith in the living

God who hears and answers prayer: "God is our refuge and strength, a very present help in trouble." (Psalms 46:1)

However, the assurance of God's care comes only to those who, like Jeremiah, have responded to the message of God, as unpopular as it might be. Jeremiah preached repentance and obedience, or judgement and captivity. Jerusalem in arrogant disregard to the message of God, refused to listen. The result was the redemption of Jeremiah from the pit, and the fall of Jerusalem to the enemy.

People in reach of God's help all too often turn aside because of pride or unbelief. The path of deliverance by God is clear: "Come now, let us reason together," says the LORD. "Though your sins are like scarlet, they shall be as white as snow; though they are red as crimson, they shall be like wool. If you are willing and obedient, you will eat the best from the land" (Isaiah 1:18-19 NIV).

As the hymn states, "Trust and obey, for there is no other way, to be happy in Jesus, but to trust and obey." In whatever state of despair you may be in, take up a Bible, absorb the message (I suggest you begin with reading the Gospel of John along with the Psalms of David), and seek the Lord's help in the spirit of true humility, as Jeremiah bid his own people: "Let us examine our ways and test them, and let us return to the LORD. Let us lift up our hearts and our hands to God in heaven, and say: "We have sinned and rebelled and you have not forgiven" (Lamentations 3:40-42 NIV).

Personal Notes

John 1:1-14

In the beginning was the Word, and the Word was with God, and the Word was God. He was in the beginning with God. All things were made through Him, and without Him nothing was made that was made. In Him was life, and the life was the light of men. And the light shines in the darkness, and the darkness did not comprehend it. There was a man sent from God, whose name was John. This man came for a witness, to bear witness of the Light, that all through him might believe. He was not that Light, but was sent to bear witness of that Light. That was the true Light which gives light to every man coming into the world. He was in the world, and the world was made through Him, and the world did not know Him. He came to His own, and His own did not receive Him. But as many as received Him, to them He gave the right to become children of God, to those who believe in His name: who were born, not of blood, nor of the will of the flesh, nor of the will of man, but of God. And the Word became flesh and dwelt among us, and we beheld His glory, the glory as of the only begotten of the Father, full of grace and truth.

The Brightness of God's Glory

For a school science project, my son and I experimented with making a telescope. Unfortunately, about the only thing we accomplished was magnifying the neighbour's porch light to just below the pain threshold of brightness. I had no idea that a porch light, when intensified with a lens could be so brilliant, especially when completely unfocussed!

Imagine the wonder of Peter, James and John when on that mount so long ago, they saw Jesus transfigured before their eyes. Imagine the awe they experienced when the Son of God cast aside the veil of His Glory and became radiant before these disciples. Scripture describes the scene: "And after six days Jesus took Peter, James, and John his brother, and brought them up into an high mountain apart, and was transfigured before them: and his face did shine as the sun, and his raiment was white as the light" (Matthew 17:1-2). These three apostles saw a spectacle far surpassing any modern laser show or special effects presentation, they saw the reflected majesty and perfected glory of God!

The Epistle of Hebrews addresses Jesus as "the brightness of His (the Father's) glory, the express image of His person" (Hebrews

98

1:23). That radiant glory penetrated the person of Moses as he stood before God, to the extent that his face shone for a while. That reflected majesty broke upon Isaiah in a vision that brought him to a repent cry: "Woe is me! for I am undone; because I am a man of unclean lips, and I dwell in the midst of a people of unclean lips: for mine eyes have seen the King, the LORD of hosts" (Isaiah 6:5).

That same glory blinded Peter, motivated Paul, and moved John in awe with these words: "That which was from the beginning, which we have heard, which we have seen with our eyes, which we have looked upon, and our hands have handled, of the Word of life; For the life was manifested, and we have seen it, and bear witness, and show unto you that eternal life, which was with the Father, and was manifested unto us" (1 John 1:1-2).

Jesus walked upon this earth fully man, and, although in a state of veiled glory, He was fully God as well. Paul declared "in him dwells all the fullness of the Godhead bodily" (Colossians 2:9). With Christmas a couple of months behind us and Easter just ahead of us, it becomes too easy to resort to the normal routine of business and bustle, and to forget that Jesus, God's Son, man's suffering, and risen Saviour, deserves our worship, our wonder, and our adoration. "O Come let us adore Him" every day of the year! Let us offer Him the sacrifice of our praise, and join with heavenly hosts in singing "Holy, holy, holy is the Lord of Hosts, the whole earth is full of His glory!" (Isaiah 6:3).

Personal Notes

1 John 1:1-7

That which was from the beginning, which we have heard, which we have seen with our eyes, which we have looked upon, and our hands have handled, concerning the Word of life— the life was manifested, and we have seen, and bear witness, and declare to you that eternal life which was with the Father and was manifested to us— that which we have seen and heard we declare to you, that you also may have fellowship with us; and truly our fellowship is with the Father and with His Son Jesus Christ. And these things we write to you that your joy may be full. This is the message which we have heard from Him and declare to you, that God is light and in Him is no darkness at all. If we say that we have fellowship with Him, and walk in darkness, we lie and do not practice the truth. But if we walk in the light as He is in the light, we have fellowship with one another, and the blood of Jesus Christ His Son cleanses us from all sin.

The Sense of Proper Pride

A great sense of pride swept over me as I watched the Canadian men's Olympic relay team burn up the track, leaving their competition in the dust. It was particularly enjoyable because at the time I was at a school in the United States, amidst a crowd of Americans who refused to believe that their team could lose. Similarly, when Paul Henderson put that puck past the Russian goal tender in the last seconds of the game for a final Canadian win in 1972, I was out of the country and had the unique privilege of sensing Canadian pride while among strangers.

That same feeling of warmth through "pride of association" should be the experience of every Christian toward the incomparable Christ. Jesus Christ is God's Son, worthy of our worship; He is the Good Shepherd, deserving of our love. He is also our Great Saviour, to whom our loyalty is due. Such loyalty, however, will not be given unless the greatness of His salvation is understood, and the greatness of Christ's salvation cannot be understood unless we first recognize the wickedness of man's soul.

Jonathan Edwards' message "Sinners in the Hands of an Angry God" may not be popular; nevertheless, it reflects God's truth. Edwards states: "Sin is the ruin and misery of the soul; it is destructive in its nature; and if God should leave it without restraint, there would need nothing else to make the soul perfectly miserable. The corruption of the heart of man is immoderate and boundless in its fury; and while wicked men live here, it is like fire pent up by the course of nature" (see Romans 1 and Psalm 51).

Secondly, the greatness of Christ's salvation cannot be appreciated without seeing the helplessness of man's state. The scripture states that "when we were yet without strength, in due time Christ died for the ungodly" (Romans 5:6). Like those poor men left buried in a collapsed mine, and the crew of a crippled submarine that went too deep, no escape was possible, so is man in attempted escape from the consequences of sin. There is no escape, there is no human hope.

Yet in man's total sinfulness and complete helplessness, the greatness of Christ's salvation is realized in the lowliness of our substitute. God's Son became sin for us: "For Christ died for sins once for all, the righteous for the unrighteous, to bring you to God" (1 Peter 3:18 NIV). Will Christians ever know the true lowliness and shame that Christ experienced on the cross as He took man's place? Will believers ever realize the agony in Christ's words "My God, My God, why have you forsaken me?"

With humble hearts, everyone who has received by faith God's gift of life, (Romans 6:23) is privileged to reflect with the warm pride of association, that Jesus Christ, in performing the greatest task of all - bearing the sins of the world, is our Great Saviour and friend. What "pride of association is the believer's privilege! Has He your loyalty?

Personal Notes

Jeremiah 12:1-6

Righteous are You, O LORD, when I plead with You; Yet let me talk with You about Your judgments. Why does the way of the wicked prosper? Why are those happy who deal so treacherously? You have planted them, yes, they have taken root; They grow, yes, they bear fruit. You are near in their mouth But far from their mind. But You, O LORD, know me; You have seen me, And You have tested my heart toward You. Pull them out like sheep for the slaughter, And prepare them for the day of slaughter. How long will the land mourn, And the herbs of every field wither? The beasts and birds are consumed, For the wickedness of those who dwell there, Because they said, "He will not see our final end." "If you have run with the footmen, and they have wearied you, Then how can you contend with horses? And if in the land of peace, In which you trusted, they wearied you, Then how will you do in the floodplain of the Jordan? For even your brothers, the house of your father, Even they have dealt treacherously with you; Yes, they have called a multitude after you. Do not believe them, Even though they speak smooth words to you.

The Christian Olympics

With the thrill of victory and agony of defeat experienced by our athletes ever fresh in our minds, it would seem appropriate to examine the scripture parallels to the Christian life. Indeed, one of the common comparisons that God uses in His Word to convey the walk of the Christian in that of the athlete. Paul in particular traces the Christian walk in term of training and competing for the prize. He states that the follower of Christ must be involved in the regular discipline of spiritual exercise: "For bodily exercise profits [a] little: but godliness is profitable unto all things, having promise of the life that now is, and of that which is to come" (1 Timothy 4:8). Paul knew the great value of the daily spiritual exercise of prayer, meditation on Scripture and determination to glorify God in every circumstance.

Added to these basic disciplines, Paul also recognized the need for each believer to practice self-discipline by turning from sin. He compares this to the athlete holding to the rules while in competition. "Know ye not that they which run in a race run all, but one receives the prize? So run, that ye may obtain. And every man that strives for the mastery is temperate in all things. Now they [do it] to obtain a corruptible crown; but we an incorruptible. I therefore so run, not as uncertainly; so fight I, not as one that beats the air: But I keep under my body, and bring [it] into subjection: lest that by any means, when I have preached to others, I myself should be a castaway" (1 Corinthians 9:24-27).

Finally, Paul was fully aware of the award ceremonies awaiting each believer, a judgement not to determine eternal destiny (this is decided for the believer in Christ, see Romans 8:1), but to determine awards. "For we must all appear before the judgment seat of Christ; that every one may receive the things done in his body, according to that he hath done, whether it be good or bad (2 Corinthians 5:10). The term Paul uses here, translated "judgment seat", is Bema, the Greek term used in athletic competition for the place where performance is graded and the winner crowned.

The truth that God wishes all Christians to grasp is clear. Although salvation is a gift from God through faith in Christ as a sacrifice for sin, the believing "Child of God" is encouraged to live for the Lord each day, valuing the reward in heaven for a surrendered life as a greater treasure than any earthly gain. This defines what a life of faith involves: "By faith Moses, when he was come to years, refused to be called the son of Pharaoh's daughter; ...Esteeming the reproach of Christ greater riches than the treasures in Egypt: for he had respect unto the recompense of the reward" (Hebrews 11:24,26). This also determines where the Christian's heart is kept: "For where your treasure is, there will your heart be also" (Matthew 6:21). Christian friend, run to win!

Personal Notes

103

1 Samuel 2:1-10

"No one is holy like the LORD, For there is none besides You, Nor is there any rock like our God. "Talk no more so very proudly; Let no arrogance come from your mouth, For the LORD is the God of knowledge; And by Him actions are weighed. "The bows of the mighty men are broken, And those who stumbled are girded with strength. Those who were full have hired themselves out for bread, And the hungry have ceased to hunger. Even the barren has borne seven, And she who has many children has become feeble. "The LORD kills and makes alive; He brings down to the grave and brings up. The LORD makes poor and makes rich; He brings low and lifts up. He raises the poor from the dust And lifts the beggar from the ash heap, To set them among princes And make them inherit the throne of glory. "For the pillars of the earth are the LORD'S, And He has set the world upon them. He will guard the feet of His saints, But the wicked shall be silent in darkness. "For by strength no man shall prevail. The adversaries of the LORD shall be broken in pieces; From heaven He will thunder against them. The LORD will judge the ends of the earth. "He will give strength to His king, And exalt the horn of His anointed."

Panic or Peace?

An uncle who had no use for worship said to his Sunday School- attending niece, "I'll give you a loonie (Canadian $1 coin) if you show me where God is." The young girl wisely responded, "I'll give you toonie (Canadian $2 coin) if you show me where God isn't."

Such childlike acceptance of God's all present and all powerful nature has slipped from the grasp of many Christians. This is evident in the apparent growing alarm that is expressed by believers regarding the "out of control" state of our world. Christian friend, our world is never out of the control of the living God. No matter how bad things seem, remember, God is sovereign. "The LORD kills, and makes alive: he brings down to the grave, and brings up. The LORD makes poor, and makes rich: he brings low, and lifts up. He raises up the poor out of the dust, and lifts up the beggar from the dunghill, to set them among princes, and to make them inherit the throne of glory: for the pillars of the earth are the LORD'S, and he hath set the world upon them" (1 Samuel 2:6-8).

God's sovereignty can be defined as the work of His rule which ensures the completion of His purpose, the execution of His judgements, and the care of His people, in accord with the fulfilment of His Word. The book of Esther is a testimony to the sovereignty of God. In this short Old Testament book in which the name of God is not even mentioned, we see God dispatching His judgement on Hamaan the Amalekite, according to His prophecy hundreds of years earlier. We see God crushing the enemies of His people, and we see God preserving His people in the midst of a wicked culture, by bringing them to repentance (Esther 4:3 - sackcloth and ashes), by focusing their attention to His promises (Esther 4:14 - deliverance shall come), and by meaningful worship (Esther 9:20 - the commencement of the feast of Purim).

God's sovereignty guarantees that even unbelieving men pursuing the wickedness of their imaginations is held within the boundaries of God's determined limits. M.R. DeHaan challenges the over wrought believer with these words: "today God is calling out a remnant... in response to the Word of God. I believe it is a sin for a Christian who knows his Bible to become greatly upset about world conditions as though God were not in control any longer."

Therefore, the believer's task is to refrain from worry: "Be anxious for nothing; but in everything by prayer and supplication with thanksgiving let your requests be made known unto God" (Philippians 4:6). The Christian's call is in trust to preach (share the gospel), to pray (for those in authority), and to plug away (looking unto Jesus the author and finisher of our faith). As the children's Sunday School song states: "Why worry when you can pray, Trust Jesus He'll be your stay, Don't be a doubting Thomas, Rest fully on His promise, Why worry, worry, worry, worry, when you can pray!"

Personal Notes

Matthew 16:13-21

When Jesus came into the coasts of Caesarea Philippi, he asked his disciples, saying, Whom do men say that I the Son of man am? And they said, Some say that thou art John the Baptist: some, Elias; and others, Jeremias, or one of the prophets. He saith unto them, But whom say ye that I am? And Simon Peter answered and said, Thou art the Christ, the Son of the living God. And Jesus answered and said unto him, Blessed art thou, Simon Barjona: for flesh and blood hath not revealed it unto thee, but my Father which is in heaven. And I say also unto thee, That thou art Peter, and upon this rock I will build my church; and the gates of hell shall not prevail against it. And I will give unto thee the keys of the kingdom of heaven: and whatsoever thou shalt bind on earth shall be bound in heaven: and whatsoever thou shalt loose on earth shall be loosed in heaven. Then charged he his disciples that they should tell no man that he was Jesus the Christ. From that time forth began Jesus to shew unto his disciples, how that he must go unto Jerusalem, and suffer many things of the elders and chief priests and scribes, and be killed, and be raised again the third day.

A Commitment Crisis

"Commitment" in our fast paced, self-centred society has been withdrawn from the domain of service and placed in the folders of humanity marked "convenience", "profit", or "security." For this reason the self-sacrificial life of Christ is seen as an anomaly, and the call to follow Him as his disciple a misunderstood principle of life.

Nevertheless, Christ did die sacrificially for the world, to provide the only means of reconciliation between God and man: "For even the Son of man came not to be ministered unto, but to minister, and to give his life a ransom for many" (Mark 10:45), "For there is one God, and one mediator between God and men, the man Christ Jesus" (1 Timothy 2:5), "Neither is there salvation in any other: for there is none other name under heaven given among men, whereby we must be saved" (Acts 4:12).

As well, Jesus did present a unique call to commitment to all those who would believe on Him: "If any man will come after me, let him deny himself, and take up his cross, and follow me" (Matthew 16:24), "And whosoever doth not bear his cross, and come after me, cannot be my disciple" (Luke 14:27). Yet Christ's church continues to struggle to find people who will serve anywhere, anytime, under any circumstances!

106

Perhaps an example of the true meaning of commitment is in order. 'Leadership' magazine, Spring '90 cites Tim Bowden, in his book *One Crowded Hour* about cameraman Neil Davis in Borneo during the confrontation between Malaysia and Indonesia in 1964. A group of Gurkhas from Nepal were asked if they would be willing to jump from transport planes into combat against the Indonesians if the need arose. The Gurkhas had the right to turn down the request because they had never been trained as paratroopers. Bowden quotes Davis's account of the story: "Now the Gurkhas usually agreed to anything, but on this occasion they provisionally rejected the plan. But the next day one of their NCO's sought out the British officer who made the request and said they had discussed the matter further and would be prepared to jump under certain conditions.

"What are they?" asked the British officer.

"The Gurkhas told him they would jump if the land was marshy or reasonably soft with no rocky outcrops, because they were inexperienced in falling. The British officer considered this, and said that the dropping area would almost certainly be over jungle, and there would not be rocky outcrops, so that seemed all right. Was there anything else?

"Yes, said the Gurkhas. They wanted the plane to fly as slowly as possible and no more than one hundred feet high. The British officer pointed out the planes always did fly as slowly as possible when dropping troops, but to jump from one hundred feet was impossible, because the parachutes would not open in time from that height.

"Oh," said the Gurkhas, "that's all right, then. We'll jump with parachutes anywhere. You didn't mention parachutes before!" Now that's commitment!

Personal Notes

Matthew 6:6-15

"And when you pray, you shall not be like the hypocrites. For they love to pray standing in the synagogues and on the corners of the streets, that they may be seen by men. Assuredly, I say to you, they have their reward. "But you, when you pray, go into your room, and when you have shut your door, pray to your Father who is in the secret place; and your Father who sees in secret will reward you openly. "And when you pray, do not use vain repetitions as the heathen do. For they think that they will be heard for their many words. "Therefore do not be like them. For your Father knows the things you have need of before you ask Him.

"In this manner, therefore, pray: Our Father in heaven, Hallowed be Your name. Your kingdom come. Your will be done On earth as it is in heaven. Give us this day our daily bread. And forgive us our debts, As we forgive our debtors. And do not lead us into temptation, But deliver us from the evil one. For Yours is the kingdom and the power and the glory forever. Amen. "For if you forgive men their trespasses, your heavenly Father will also forgive you. "But if you do not forgive men their trespasses, neither will your Father forgive your trespasses.

The Great Delusion

In O. Henry's book, *The Gentle Grafter*, the author presents people as easy prey for the con-artist. His stories are often humorous; however, the truth of man's vulnerability cannot be laughed at, especially when eternity is at stake. Scripture tells us that Satan has "blinded the minds of unbelievers, so that they cannot see the light of the glorious gospel of Christ." How true this is. Even in Canada, most people believe that by living a good life, or obeying the Ten Commandments, or by some other means, they can earn salvation. This is Satan's most successful delusion, because it preys upon the pride of man.

The Bible makes it very clear, man does not deserve heaven, nor can he earn heaven; "For by grace are we saved through faith and that not of ourselves, it is the gift of God, not of works, lest any man should boast." Here scripture states that salvation is by God's grace. Grace implies a favour freely offered, something given yet completely undeserved. Here also, the Bible tells us that salvation is a gift. This implies something given out of love, something certainly unearned.

The only involvement that man has in securing heaven is the response of repentance and faith: Repentance that senses sorrow because of sin, Faith that believes Christ paid the penalty of sin on the cross and rose from the dead to certify such claim and Faith that calls on Christ in prayer to be personal Saviour.

Satan is no gentle grafter, he is a powerful spirit being opposed to God, who seeks by lies and deception to keep men from the salvation freely offered by a loving Lord. He is not, as some would tell us, a fictitious expression of man's imagination, but a deadly foe, imitating God even to the extent of establishing his own church. He is the Devil - accuser or adversary - Matt. 4:1-8; He is the Tempter - Matt. 4:3, 1 Thess. 3:5; He is Beelzebub - Prince of the Demons - Matt. 12:24; He is the Enemy - Matt. 13:39, He is the Evil One - Matt. 13:19,38; 1 John 13:14; 3:12; 5:18, He is Belial - Pertains to worthlessness - II Cor. 6:15; He is the Adversary - one who opposes - 1 Peter 5:8; He is the Deceiver - Rev. 12:9; He is the Father of Lies - John 8:44; He is a Murderer - John 8:44; He is the Sinner - 1 John 3:8. Satan has two basic goals: to convince the unsaved that they are saved and to convince the saved that they are unsaved. Christ taught His disciples to pray for deliverance from Satan (the Evil One). Therefore, "Be sober, be vigilant; because your adversary the devil, as a roaring lion, walks about, seeking whom he may devour: Whom resist steadfast in the faith" (1 Peter 5:8-9).

Personal Notes

February 23

Ephesians 4:20-32

But you have not so learned Christ, if indeed you have heard Him and have been taught by Him, as the truth is in Jesus: that you put off, concerning your former conduct, the old man which grows corrupt according to the deceitful lusts, and be renewed in the spirit of your mind, and that you put on the new man which was created according to God, in true righteousness and holiness. Therefore, putting away lying, "Let each one of you speak truth with his neighbour," for we are members of one another. "Be angry, and do not sin": do not let the sun go down on your wrath, nor give place to the devil. Let him who stole steal no longer, but rather let him labour, working with his hands what is good, that he may have something to give him who has need. Let no corrupt word proceed out of your mouth, but what is good for necessary edification, that it may impart grace to the hearers. And do not grieve the Holy Spirit of God, by whom you were sealed for the day of redemption. Let all bitterness, wrath, anger, clamour, and evil speaking be put away from you, with all malice. And be kind to one another, tenderhearted, forgiving one another, just as God in Christ forgave you.

Silver Box Believers

Painter Benjamin West tells how he loved to paint as a youngster. When his mother left, he would pull out the oils and try to paint. One day he pulled out all the paints and made quite a mess. He hoped to get it all cleaned up before his mother came back. But she came and discovered the mess. West said what she did next completely surprised him. She picked up his painting and said, "My, what a beautiful painting of your sister." She gave him a kiss on the cheek and walked away. With that kiss, West says, he became a painter.

Every day Christians are trying to paint the picture of Jesus in their lives through what is said and done. But messes are often made. The last thing needed is for fellow believers to come along and say, "What a mess!" What we need is a kiss of encouragement. It's vital for life and for relationships. Paul called the Christians at Galatia to the ministry of encouragement. He wrote: "Brethren, if a man be overtaken in a fault, you who are spiritual restore such a one in the spirit of meekness, considering yourself, lest you also be tempted. Bear one another's burdens, and so fulfil the law of Christ." (Gal 6:1)

So important is the ministry of encouragement that one of the spiritual gifts (a special ability endowed by the Spirit of God at salvation) is designated in scripture as such: "Having then gifts differing according to the grace that is given to us, whether prophecy, let us prophesy according to the proportion of faith;   Or ministry, let us wait on our ministering: or he that teaches, on teaching;   Or he that exhorts, on exhortation" (Romans 12:6-8). The term exhortation is *paraklesis*, meaning 'a calling near, summons especially for help, or an exhortation, admonition of encouragement.'

Think about David Livingstone when he climbed into the pulpit of a little church in Scotland. He'd honed his sermon. He'd prepared it so very well. He wanted to be a great preacher. He wanted to go give his life on the mission field. And when he got up to preach that night, he flapped his wings, but he couldn't get off the runway. He tried, but finally he forgot his sermon altogether; so he apologized to the people and left in great shame.

But Robert Moffat, the famous missionary, was there. And Moffat came up to him after the service and said, "You can be a great and wonderful servant of God. Why don't you go to medical school?" Today you can't mention Africa without thinking about David Livingstone. But what would have happened to David Livingstone without Robert Moffat?

Florence Littauer, in *Today's Christian Woman*, wrote: "On the spur of the moment, I was asked to give a children's sermon in a church I was visiting. My mind raced to Ephesians 4:29: "Let no corrupt communication proceed out of your mouth, but that which is good ..."

I asked the children, "How can we make our words good for others?" They answered, "Say nice things. give out compliments. Be cheerful. Tell the truth."

Then a little girl piped up, "Our words should be like little silver boxes with bows on top."

What more could I say? The children had taught the verse to each other and to me in a way none of us could easily forget. Christian friend, are you a silver box believer?

Personal Notes

111

Isaiah 40:27-31

Why do you say, O Jacob, And speak, O Israel: "My way is hidden from the LORD, And my just claim is passed over by my God"? Have you not known? Have you not heard? The everlasting God, the LORD, The Creator of the ends of the earth, Neither faints nor is weary. His understanding is unsearchable. He gives power to the weak, And to those who have no might He increases strength. Even the youths shall faint and be weary, And the young men shall utterly fall, But those who wait on the LORD Shall renew their strength; They shall mount up with wings like eagles, They shall run and not be weary, They shall walk and not faint.

Eagle's Wings

"See how the eagle mounts! Does it care for the ethereal blue, or aspire to commune with the stars of heaven? Not a whit; such airy considerations have no weight with the ravenous bird, and yet you will not wonder that it soars aloft when you remember that it thus obtains a broader range of vision and so becomes more able to provide for its nest... Wonder not that people with the hearts of devils yet mount like angels: there is a reason that explains it all" (Charles Haddon Spurgeon).

The heart in Biblical poetry is that inner part of man which constitutes his spirit and soul and frames his mind, inclinations, and emotions, it is the "real you." There are four distinct heart conditions suggested in the book of Proverbs. There is the dying heart, contrasted with the living heart, and there is the troubled heart contrasted with the triumphant heart. The troubled heart is heavy with worry (Prov. 25:20), immersed in sorrow (Prov. 14:13), filled with envy (Prov. 23:17), yet often too proud to admit its condition and cry to God for help: "Before his downfall a man's heart is proud, but humility comes before honour" (Proverbs 18:12 NIV).

In contrast to the troubled heart, the triumphant heart is merry, creating a cheerful countenance (Prov. 15:13), its rejoicing puts a glimmer of light in the eye (Prov. 15:30). The triumphant heart is sound in the confidence of God's plan and care and therefore, finds life in fulness, and freedom from envy (Prov. 14:30). The triumphant heart has passed from trouble by first humbling itself before God in simple trust: "He that is of a proud heart stirreth up strife: but he that putteth his trust in the LORD shall be made fat. He that trusteth in his own heart is a fool: but whoso walketh wisely, he shall be delivered" (Proverbs 28:25-26).

There is a reason that men with "hearts of devils" are able to "mount like eagles." The reason is DEPENDENCE ON GOD. Proverbs states this in terms of believing obedience: "My son, forget not my law; but let thine heart keep my commandments: For length of days, and long life, and peace, shall they add to thee" (Proverbs 3:1-2). Joshua spoke of this in terms of careful allegiance: "This book of the law shall not depart out of thy mouth; but thou shalt meditate therein day and night, that thou mayest observe to do according to all that is written therein: for then thou shalt make thy way prosperous, and successful" (Joshua 1:8). Christ spoke of this in terms of spiritual diet: "Man shall not live by bread alone, but by every word that proceedeth out of the mouth of God" (Matthew 4:4).

Isaiah spoke of this as the soaring eagle: "But they that wait upon the LORD shall renew their strength; they shall mount up with wings as eagles; they shall run, and not be weary; and they shall walk, and not faint" (Isaiah 40:31). Friend, does your heart soar or swoon?

Personal Notes

Proverbs 6:12-19

A worthless person, a wicked man, Walks with a perverse mouth; He winks with his eyes, He shuffles his feet, He points with his fingers; Perversity is in his heart, He devises evil continually, He sows discord. Therefore his calamity shall come suddenly; Suddenly he shall be broken without remedy. These six things the LORD hates, Yes, seven are an abomination to Him: A proud look, A lying tongue, Hands that shed innocent blood, A heart that devises wicked plans, Feet that are swift in running to evil, A false witness who speaks lies, And one who sows discord among brethren.

Unzipping the Heart

"They might not look like they have much in common, the 74 year-old and his 4 year-old grandson, but they do. You'll see the similarity on a hot summer day when they peel off their T-shirts to go swimming: Each has a long dramatic scar running the length of his chest. Danny, the 4 year-old, actually got his scar after major corrective heart surgery following his 1st birthday. His grandfather got his last year after emergency open-heart bypass surgery. Swapping scar stories one day, Danny asked his Grandpa, "Do you think the doctors gave us a zipper on our chests so Jesus could get into our heart easier?" Leave it to a child to turn a traumatic event into a picture of faith. And while Danny's theological understanding reflects his age, his cute words carry a pointed challenge." (From *Christian Parenting*, November/December, 1996).

The heart in Biblical poetry, is that inner part of man which constitutes his spirit and soul and frames his mind, inclinations, and emotions, it is the "real you." God addresses the health of the heart in terms of its diet and exercise. Scripture urges believers to CURB THE DIET OF THE HEART by eliminating garbage "soul" food. The heart (mind) that diets on wicked imaginations (Prov. 6:18) and dwells on lust (Prov. 6:25) will continue to slip into the bondage of sin.

In contrast, the heart that seeks a good "soul" diet of God's knowledge, understanding and wisdom finds spiritual health: "My son, if you accept my words and store up my commands within you... Then shalt thou understand the fear of the LORD, and find the knowledge of God... For wisdom will enter your heart, and knowledge will be pleasant to your soul. Discretion will protect you, and understanding will guard you" (Proverbs 2:1,5,10-11 NIV).

As well as diet control, Scripture calls the believer to MAINTAIN THE EXERCISE OF THE HEART by strengthening life's grip on God's Word: "Let thine heart *retain* my Words" (Prov. 4:4), and by building spiritual endurance through meditating on God's truth (Prov. 15:28). In essence, a believer must practice LONG TERM HEART CARE. Proverbs speaks of this in terms of *guarding the heart*: "Keep thy heart with all diligence; for out of it are the issues of life" (Proverbs 4:23), and *guiding the heart*: "Hear thou, my son, and be wise, and guide thine heart in the way" (Proverbs 23:19).

Charles Wesley portrayed the healthy heart with these words: "A heart in every thought renewed - And full of love divine, - Perfect and right and pure and good, - A copy, Lord, of thine." A French soldier who had served ably in Napoleon's army lay dying of a wound received in battle. As they probed his shattered ribs to find the fatal bullet he said, "Dig a little deeper and you will find the emperor." Christian friend, could the same be said of the emperor of your heart? How "easily unzipped" is your heart to the things of God?

Personal Notes

115

Proverbs 10:24-32

The fear of the wicked will come upon him, And the desire of the righteous will be granted. When the whirlwind passes by, the wicked is no more, But the righteous has an everlasting foundation. As vinegar to the teeth and smoke to the eyes, So is the lazy man to those who send him. The fear of the LORD prolongs days, But the years of the wicked will be shortened.

The hope of the righteous will be gladness, But the expectation of the wicked will perish. The way of the LORD is strength for the upright, But destruction will come to the workers of iniquity. The righteous will never be removed, But the wicked will not inhabit the earth. The mouth of the righteous brings forth wisdom, But the perverse tongue will be cut out. The lips of the righteous know what is acceptable, But the mouth of the wicked what is perverse.

The Tongue

Sherman Burford observed "On September 11, 1995, a squirrel climbed on the Metro-North Railroad power lines near New York City. This set off an electrical surge, which weakened an overhead bracket, which let a wire dangle toward the tracks, which tangled in a train, which tore down all the lines. As a result, 47,000 commuters were stuck in Manhattan."

Like that small squirrel that caused so much trouble, the tongue is also small but has the power of destruction. God's wisdom literature of Proverbs defines both the corrupted tongue and the transformed tongue. The corrupted tongue is a destructive fire. "An ungodly man plans evil, and his tongue is like a burning fire" (Proverbs 16:27).

The corrupted tongue is like a snare that traps the speaker in sin (Proverbs 12:13). It has the destructive power to injure others deeply (Proverbs 12:18), to crush the spirit (Proverbs 15:4), to corrupt life (Proverbs 17:20), waste life (Proverbs 21:6), impoverish life (Proverbs 25:23), and altogether ruin life (Proverbs 26:28). Indeed, this anonymous poem states the matter of the destructive power of the tongue well: "The boneless tongue, so small and weak, Can crush and kill," declares the Greek. "The tongue destroys a greater horde," the Turk asserts, "than does the sword." The Persian proverb wisely says, "A lengthy tongue--an early death!" - or sometimes takes this form instead, "Don't let your tongue cut off your head."

In contrast, the transformed tongue can be a ministering force: "The mouth of the righteous brings forth wisdom" (Proverbs 10:31 NIV). This is a tongue that has the potential to strengthen (Proverbs 12:18), to even bring spiritual life (Proverbs 15:4). The transformed tongue has the potential to captivate enemies and persuade a foe (Proverbs 25:15). It can deliver spiritual and psychological nourishment. This is a tongue that can discern what is acceptable to state (Proverbs 10:32), what is good advice (Proverbs 15:7), while at the same time be able to guard against trouble (Proverbs 21:23) and stimulate a thirst for knowledge (Proverbs 16:21).

The grace that grows from personal trust in Christ as Saviour, seasons the tongue and transforms it from a destructive fire to a ministering force. The transformation is accomplished by the work of God in a life that understands the dependant priority. This priority is first a promise to be kept by the believer: "I will speak of excellent things; and the opening of my lips shall be right things. For my mouth shall speak truth; and wickedness is an abomination to my lips" (Proverbs 8:6-7). It is a promise that says: "I will only speak words befitting the language of my country (heaven), the character of my transformation (righteousness), and the nature of my king (to love truth and hate evil). This priority is also a commitment to a law that rules the tongue: "...in her tongue is the law of kindness" (Proverbs 31:26). This is a commitment to speak the truth in love: "...be ye kind one to another, tenderhearted, forgiving one another, even as God for Christ's sake hath forgiven you" (Ephesians 4:31-32). Is your tongue a destroying fire or ministering force?

Personal Notes

2 Thessalonians 3:6-16

But we command you, brethren, in the name of our Lord Jesus Christ, that you withdraw from every brother who walks disorderly and not according to the tradition which he received from us. For you yourselves know how you ought to follow us, for we were not disorderly among you; nor did we eat anyone's bread free of charge, but worked with labour and toil night and day, that we might not be a burden to any of you, not because we do not have authority, but to make ourselves an example of how you should follow us. For even when we were with you, we commanded you this: If anyone will not work, neither shall he eat. For we hear that there are some who walk among you in a disorderly manner, not working at all, but are busybodies. Now those who are such we command and exhort through our Lord Jesus Christ that they work in quietness and eat their own bread. But as for you, brethren, do not grow weary in doing good. And if anyone does not obey our word in this epistle, note that person and do not keep company with him, that he may be ashamed. Yet do not count him as an enemy, but admonish him as a brother.

God's Honour Role

There was an article in the *Readers Digest* a few years ago about a public school principal in a tough neighbourhood of Edmonton who turned the attitude of the students completely around. His method was not one of rebuke, but one of reward. He invented "honour rolls" for just about every imaginable achievement possible. As a result, practically every child had opportunity to be recognized for some achievement.

It would seem that once the students saw the principal as a passionate person as well as an authority figure, he was able to gain their confidence. In so doing he won the respect of the neighbourhood and his positive influence extended far beyond the school ground.

Our world needs to see the Lord God in that same way, not only as supreme in authority but as deep in passion. To do so the Lord has established His own "honour roll". The list begins in Hebrews 11 where God recognizes Abel, Enoch, Noah, Abraham and Sarah, Isaac, Jacob, Joseph, Moses, and many others. The criteria for making the honour roll is *faith* alone, and the Lord makes it clear that the list is still being added to: "But without faith [it is] impossible to please

[him]: for he that cometh to God must believe that he is, and [that] he is a rewarder of them that diligently seek him" (Hebrews 11:6).

Let all those who, by faith, have come to know Christ as personal Saviour and who by faith have turned their attention to the will of God rather than self-interest, know that He rewards. For all who have faced rebuke, ridicule, and even rejection because of the choice to "love the Lord your God with all your heart and with all your soul and with all your mind" (Matthew 22:37), God has an honour roll that will last through eternity. Be reminded of these closing words of scripture: "And, behold, I come quickly; and my reward [is] with me, to give every man according as his work shall be" (Revelation 22:12).

The Lord calls each believer to take up his or her cross daily (Luke 9:23). For some this means heartache, for others, ceaseless care, and still others, great burden. Yet in all this, God ensures each Christian of this promise: "God is not unjust; he will not forget your work and the love you have shown him as you have helped his people and continue to help them" (Hebrews 6:10 NIV). For this reason the attitude of the believer should always be as Paul's: "For our light and momentary troubles are achieving for us an eternal glory that far outweighs them all. So we fix our eyes not on what is seen, but on what is unseen. For what is seen is temporary, but what is unseen is eternal. (2 Corinthians 4:17-18 NIV).

With God's honour list in view, let every committed Christian determine not to grow weary in well-doing!

Personal Notes

Ephesians 1:3-12

Blessed be the God and Father of our Lord Jesus Christ, who has blessed us with every spiritual blessing in the heavenly places in Christ, just as He chose us in Him before the foundation of the world, that we should be holy and without blame before Him in love, having predestined us to adoption as sons by Jesus Christ to Himself, according to the good pleasure of His will, to the praise of the glory of His grace, by which He has made us accepted in the Beloved. In Him we have redemption through His blood, the forgiveness of sins, according to the riches of His grace which He made to abound toward us in all wisdom and prudence, having made known to us the mystery of His will, according to His good pleasure which He purposed in Himself, that in the dispensation of the fullness of the times He might gather together in one all things in Christ, both which are in heaven and which are on earth—in Him. In Him also we have obtained an inheritance, being predestined according to the purpose of Him who works all things according to the counsel of His will, that we who first trusted in Christ should be to the praise of His glory.

Rags to Riches

In the original story from Arabian Nights, Aladdin was not nearly as sharp as the Aladdin of the recent children's cartoon. The original lad, after discovering the secret of a magic lamp and a magic ring, chose to continue in poverty and hunger even though unlimited wealth was a wish away. That pattern is lived out in countless lives every day by Christians who have man's most precious possession - salvation, yet neglect its sustaining value.

Peter addressed the great wealth of salvation in these words: "Praise be to the God and Father of our Lord Jesus Christ! In his great mercy he has given us new birth into a living hope through the resurrection of Jesus Christ from the dead, To an inheritance incorruptible, and undefiled, and that fades not away, reserved in heaven for you, Who are kept by the power of God through faith unto salvation ready to be revealed in the last time." (1 Peter 1:3-5) Consider the sustaining value of the three treasures of salvation mentioned here.

First there is the treasure of awakening to a living hope. Religions seek to offer the hope of good morals, strong disciplines, or ordered living, but they are as dead as their leaders. Salvation in Christ is a new hope within, the operating presence of a risen, living Saviour: "God has chosen to make known among the Gentiles the glorious riches of this mystery, which is Christ in you, the hope of glory." (Colossians 1:27 NIV)

Second, there is the treasure of gaining of a lasting inheritance. This inheritance is all the glory of the eternal kingdom, a joy of which will never grow stale but become newer every day. This inheritance is so spectacular that man cannot wrap his mind around it, therefore God just described it in terms of what it is not; it is untouchable by enemies, unstainable by sin, and unimpaired by time. The Lord also describes the environment of this inheritance in terms of absences; no pain, no sorrow, no separation, no death (see Revelation 21:1-4).

Third, salvation's treasure is to be kept by a limitless protection. Although salvation's ultimate end is still a drawn curtain, God's guarantee that not one of His own will miss the debut is so sure that He speaks of it as already complete. The believer's safekeeping is so certain that Christ has already prepared a home, specifically designed with each child in view (See John 14:1-3), and the dinner table is already set for the feast (see Luke 14:15-24).

Aladdin remained in a state of poverty until love got hold of his heart and caused him to pursue the riches at his disposal. Should not God's love turn the Christian's attention to the riches of salvation as well? "How great is the love the Father has lavished on us, that we should be called children of God! And that is what we are!"(1 John 3:1 NIV). Christian friend, don't ignore your greatest riches!

Personal Notes

121

Luke 8:5-15

"A sower went out to sow his seed. And as he sowed, some fell by the wayside; and it was trampled down, and the birds of the air devoured it. "Some fell on rock; and as soon as it sprang up, it withered away because it lacked moisture. "And some fell among thorns, and the thorns sprang up with it and choked it. "But others fell on good ground, sprang up, and yielded a crop a hundredfold." When He had said these things He cried, "He who has ears to hear, let him hear!" Then His disciples asked Him, saying, "What does this parable mean?" And He said, "To you it has been given to know the mysteries of the kingdom of God, but to the rest it is given in parables, that 'Seeing they may not see, And hearing they may not understand.' "Now the parable is this: The seed is the word of God. "Those by the wayside are the ones who hear; then the devil comes and takes away the word out of their hearts, lest they should believe and be saved. "But the ones on the rock are those who, when they hear, receive the word with joy; and these have no root, who believe for a while and in time of temptation fall away. "Now the ones that fell among thorns are those who, when they have heard, go out and are choked with cares, riches, and pleasures of life, and bring no fruit to maturity. "But the ones that fell on the good ground are those who, having heard the word with a noble and good heart, keep it and bear fruit with patience.

The Seed of the Gospel

"Cast your bread upon the waters, for after many days you will find it again. Give portions to seven, yes to eight, for you do not know what disaster may come upon the land." (Ecclesiastes 11:1-2). In Bible lands there is a unique way of sowing seed. The farmer floods a small field then scatters his seed on the water, as the soil absorbs the water, the seed settles into the soil awaiting the sun and time to germinate. For the poor, the grain in the home used for making bread is the very source of seed for the field. The farmer literally takes the bread (grain for bread) from the table and by faith sows it on the water in hope of an abundant harvest.

There are two ways of treating the seed. The botanist splits it up and discourses on its curious characteristics. The simple farmer eats and sows, sows and eats. Similarly there are two ways of treating the gospel. A critic dissects it, raises a mountain of debate about the structure of the whole, and relation of its parts, and when he is done with his argument, he is done. To him the letter is dead. He neither lives on it himself, nor spreads it for the good of his neighbours; he neither eats nor sows. The disciple of Jesus, hungering for righteousness, takes the seed whole; it is bread for today's hunger, and seed for tomorrow's supply.

Both the sowing of the seed of the gospel (the message of free salvation through the death, burial and resurrection of God's perfect sacrifice - His own Son) and the receiving of the seed of the gospel, is a matter of faith. For those privileged to experience new birth by faith in Christ, the sowing is a matter of duty as the salt and light of the earth (Matt. 5), and a matter of joy because God has promised an increase; "He that goes forth with weeping, bearing precious seed, shall doubtless come again with rejoicing, bringing his sheaves with him. (Psalm 126:6). For those receiving the seed is a matter of wonder and joy in new found life, hope and purpose: "Therefore, if anyone is in Christ, he is a new creation; old things have passed away; behold, all things have become new." (2 Cor. 5:17).

God's passion in this great work of sowing and reaping was clearly stated by Jesus. "Therefore said he unto them, The harvest truly is great, but the labourers are few: pray ye therefore the Lord of the harvest, that he would send forth labourers into his harvest." (Luke 10:2). It's almost impossible to see a rainbow and not point it out to someone else. It's the kind of thing that just must be shared. You see one and you want to tell someone about it. If you are by yourself and see one, it's frustrating. The gospel is such a beautiful expression of God's love that it just must be shared.

Personal Notes

Jeremiah 17:12-18

A glorious high throne from the beginning Is the place of our sanctuary. O LORD, the hope of Israel, All who forsake You shall be ashamed. "Those who depart from Me Shall be written in the earth, Because they have forsaken the LORD, The fountain of living waters." Heal me, O LORD, and I shall be healed; Save me, and I shall be saved, For You are my praise. Indeed they say to me, "Where is the word of the LORD? Let it come now!" As for me, I have not hurried away from being a shepherd who follows You, Nor have I desired the woeful day; You know what came out of my lips; It was right there before You. Do not be a terror to me; You are my hope in the day of doom. Let them be ashamed who persecute me, But do not let me be put to shame; Let them be dismayed, But do not let me be dismayed. Bring on them the day of doom, And destroy them with double destruction!

Hope Towers Above All

Hope for many is nothing more than wishful thinking that will never be realized. Benjamin Franklin said, "He that lives upon hope will die fasting." Omar Khayyam said, "It is like snow in the desert." It has also been said that "hope is a quivering, nervous creature trying to be bright and cheerful but, alas, frequently sick with nervous prostration and heart failure." On the other hand, the Bible speaks of hope as an anchor. "God wanted to make the unchanging nature of his purpose very clear to the heirs of what was promised, he confirmed it with an oath. God did this so that, by two unchangeable things in which it is impossible for God to lie, we who have fled to take hold of the hope offered to us may be greatly encouraged. We have this hope as an anchor for the soul, firm and secure." (Hebrews 6:16-19).

Unlike wishful thinking, Biblical hope is founded upon the promises of Almighty God who sent His Son to provide reconciliation for man through faith in the Son's sacrifice for sin. Biblical hope, therefore, is viewed as Jesus Himself, God's Son raised from the dead and sitting at the right hand of the Father. As a living anchor who is God himself, He is sure (unbreakable) and steadfast (unmovable) because He is our risen, eternal High Priest. . Raymond MacKendree explains: "The resurrection of Jesus Christ is our hope today. It is our assurance that we have a living Saviour to help us live as we should now, and that when, in the end, we set forth on that last great journey, we shall not travel an uncharted course, but rather we shall go on a planned voyage-life to death to eternal living."

In northern Scotland there is a mountain called Ben Hope. In the Gaelic language of Scotland "Ben" means "a mountain peak". Certainly, hope towers above all the other intangibles of life. We can live without love. We can live without faith. We can live without friends. But we cannot live without hope. Clare Booth wrote, "There are no hopeless situations; there are only men who have grown hopeless about them." In a world where hopelessness breeds in every political theatre, abounds on every street corner, and breaks the spirit of man in most homes, Christ offers a true and lasting hope.

And how, you might ask, is this hope gained? God has made His Hope simple enough for a child to find. "Jesus said to her, "I am the resurrection and the life. He who believes in me will live [have everlasting life]. (John 11:25). "Hope is the "inseparable companion" of faith. ... Without faith's knowledge of Christ, hope becomes a utopia and remains hanging in the air. But without hope, faith falls to pieces, becomes a faint-hearted and ultimately a dead faith. It is through faith that man finds the path of true life, but it is only hope that keeps him on that path. (Jurgen Moltmann). And that hope is Christ.

Personal Notes

125

1 Corinthians 3:6-20

I planted, Apollos watered, but God gave the increase. So then neither he who plants is anything, nor he who waters, but God who gives the increase. Now he who plants and he who waters are one, and each one will receive his own reward according to his own labor. For we are God's fellow workers; you are God's field, you are God's building. According to the grace of God which was given to me, as a wise master builder I have laid the foundation, and another builds on it. But let each one take heed how he builds on it. For no other foundation can anyone lay than that which is laid, which is Jesus Christ. Now if anyone builds on this foundation with gold, silver, precious stones, wood, hay, straw, each one's work will become clear; for the Day will declare it, because it will be revealed by fire; and the fire will test each one's work, of what sort it is. If anyone's work which he has built on it endures, he will receive a reward. If anyone's work is burned, he will suffer loss; but he himself will be saved, yet so as through fire. Do you not know that you are the temple of God and that the Spirit of God dwells in you? 17 If anyone defiles the temple of God, God will destroy him. For the temple of God is holy, which temple you are. Let no one deceive himself. If anyone among you seems to be wise in this age, let him become a fool that he may become wise. For the wisdom of this world is foolishness with God. For it is written, "He catches the wise in their own craftiness"; and again, "The LORD knows the thoughts of the wise, that they are futile."

Making Life Count

In updating his computer system a friend of mine lost four years of work by mistakenly saving the wrong file. When I asked him if he had "backed-up" his work, there was a long, painful pause which gave me his answer. Imagine losing four years of work with a single push of a button! Imagine the agony of mind that such a mistake would bring! Imagine how often since that mistake my friend has asked himself, "Why didn't I follow instructions and back-up my work?"

As heart-wrenching as this must have been, a worse fate awaits the negligent Christian. Paul warns of a time when every believer will stand before Christ and either have something to show for a life or lose it all. "If any man builds on this foundation using gold, silver, costly stones, wood, hay or straw, his work will be shown for what it is, because the Day will bring it to light. It will be revealed with fire, and the fire will test the quality of each man's work. If what he has built survives, he will receive his reward. If it is burned up, he will suffer loss; he himself will be saved, but only as one escaping through the flames." (1 Corinthians 3:12-15 NIV).

This is clearly not a judgment of sin. God's promise to the person who has accepted Christ as personal Saviour is removal of all condemnation (Romans 8:1), without any separation (Romans 8:31-38). However, because God has called each believer to serve Him as the salt and light of the world (the agents to bring the message of salvation through Christ to the world and the models of that new life in Christ before the world – Matthew 5), God will measure the faithfulness of His children when He calls them to His presence. Here there will be either joyful celebration at God's approval or shameful regret for a wasted life. As stewards, God will hold each believer accountable!

Should this judgment bring fear and anxiety to the believer? No – not if that life is daily surrendered to Christ. In daily surrender, the Christian makes himself/herself available to be used of God, and is empowered by God for each days tasks. The beauty of this arrangement is the wonderful fellowship the believer has with God through the process of surrendered service. This is the reality of the abundant life Christ promised.

William Booth, founder of the Salvation Army, was interviewed near the close of his life. This is what he said: "God had all there was of me. There have been others who had greater plans, greater opportunities than I; but from the day I got a vision of what God could do, I made up my mind God would have all there was of William Booth." Christian friend, has God got all of you every day? If not, you risk standing before the one who died for you empty and ashamed. There is still time to "back-up" and save your life for Christ.

Personal Notes

Psalm 51:7-19

Purge me with hyssop, and I shall be clean; Wash me, and I shall be whiter than snow. Make me hear joy and gladness, That the bones You have broken may rejoice. Hide Your face from my sins, And blot out all my iniquities. Create in me a clean heart, O God, And renew a steadfast spirit within me. Do not cast me away from Your presence, And do not take Your Holy Spirit from me. Restore to me the joy of Your salvation, And uphold me by Your generous Spirit. Then I will teach transgressors Your ways, And sinners shall be converted to You.
Deliver me from the guilt of bloodshed, O God, The God of my salvation, And my tongue shall sing aloud of Your righteousness. O Lord, open my lips, And my mouth shall show forth Your praise. For You do not desire sacrifice, or else I would give it; You do not delight in burnt offering. The sacrifices of God are a broken spirit, A broken and a contrite heart—These, O God, You will not despise. Do good in Your good pleasure to Zion; Build the walls of Jerusalem. Then You shall be pleased with the sacrifices of righteousness, With burnt offering and whole burnt offering; Then they shall offer bulls on Your altar.

Healthy Brokenness

In his message entitled *The Inadequacy of Instant Christianity*, A.W. Tozer wrote: "By "instant Christianity" I mean the kind… which is born of the notion that we may discharge our total obligation to our own souls by one act of faith, or at most two, and be relieved thereafter of all anxiety about our spiritual condition and that there is no reason to seek to be saints in character." In a society used to instant information, instant food and even instant banking, instant Christianity becomes the pursuit of many. Because salvation is a free gift from God by faith in Christ's death for man's sin, burial and resurrection, "instant Christianity" even sounds appropriate. After all, the thief on the cross beside Christ was granted salvation upon His own expression of faith.

A closer examination of Scripture would reveal that "instant Christianity" overlooks a vital element of true, saving faith – repentance. "Repent, then, and turn to God, so that your sins may be wiped out, that times of refreshing may come from the Lord." (Acts 3:19). It was only after a period of mocking Jesus along with the other criminal, that the thief had a change of heart. Perhaps as he viewed Jesus' agonizing death for sin, perhaps as he heard Jesus' words of comfort and forgiveness to others, perhaps simply because he knew that Jesus was condemned unjustly. Whatever God used to move him, the thief had a genuine change of heart. As his life was about to expire, his attention was drawn to Jesus, and with remorse for his own life and faith in Christ he cried: "Lord, remember me when you come into your kingdom."

David said: "The sacrifices of God are a broken spirit: a broken and a contrite heart, O God, thou wilt not despise." (Psalm 51:17). Vance Havner wrote: "God uses broken things. It takes broken soil to produce a crop, broken clouds to give rain, broken grain to give bread, broken bread to give strength. It is the broken alabaster box that gives forth perfume--it is Peter, weeping bitterly, who returns to greater power than ever." The faith that takes salvation's gift is rooted in the soil of a broken heart before God. Jesus reminded his disciples that it is the "poor in spirit" who find the kingdom of God. Of his ministry Jesus said: "The Spirit of the Lord GOD is upon me; because the LORD has anointed me to preach good tidings unto the meek; he has sent me to bind up the brokenhearted, to proclaim liberty to the captives, and the opening of the prison to them that are bound" (Isaiah 61:1).

There is no substitute for a broken, repentant heart. Out of it the cry of faith is born, in it the seed of new life is sown, from it the fruit of the spirit is raised and a new man is created in the image of Christ. Friend, don't seek instant Christianity, seek a broken heart, this is the workplace of God.

Personal Notes

Psalm 19:7-14

The law of the LORD is perfect, converting the soul; The testimony of the LORD is sure, making wise the simple; The statutes of the LORD are right, rejoicing the heart; The commandment of the LORD is pure, enlightening the eyes; The fear of the LORD is clean, enduring forever; The judgments of the LORD are true and righteous altogether. More to be desired are they than gold, Yea, than much fine gold; Sweeter also than honey and the honeycomb. Moreover by them Your servant is warned, And in keeping them there is great reward. Who can understand his errors? Cleanse me from secret faults. Keep back Your servant also from presumptuous sins; Let them not have dominion over me. Then I shall be blameless, And I shall be innocent of great transgression. Let the words of my mouth and the meditation of my heart Be acceptable in Your sight, O LORD, my strength and my Redeemer.

Power to Change

The great disharmony among "Christian" denominations can, for the most part, be historically traced to the parting of the ways on one major doctrine: the doctrine of the inspiration of Scripture. The Bible states: "All Scripture is given by inspiration of God and is profitable for doctrine for reproof for correction for instruction and righteousness" (2 Timothy 3:16). The word "inspiration" here, literally means "God-breathed" and defines a final written product that is the very Word of God, produced by the leading of the Holy Spirit upon godly believers, with the result of an infallible body of written documents from beginning to end. Jesus Himself attested to this in stating: "For verily I say unto you, Till heaven and earth pass, one jot or one tittle shall in no wise pass from the law, till all be fulfilled." (Matt. 5:18). This is the position of fundamental Christianity and the point of departure of many denominations.

Kirsop Lake, New Testament professor at the University of Chicago stated: "It is a mistake often made by educated persons who happen to have but little knowledge of historical theology, to suppose that fundamentalism is a new and strange form of thought. It is nothing of the kind; it is the partial and uneducated survival of a theology which was once universally held by all Christians. How many were there, for instance, in Christian churches in the 18th century who doubted the infallible inspiration of all Scripture? A few perhaps, but very few. "

George D. Barry traces the historical departure from the doctrine of inspiration: "The fact that for fifteen centuries no attempt was made to formulate a definition of the doctrine of inspiration of the Bible, testifies to the universal belief of the Church that the Scriptures were the handiwork of the Holy Spirit...It was, to our modern judgment, a mechanical and erroneous view of inspiration that was accepted and taught by the Church of the first centuries.." Scripture states: "For the Word of God is living and powerful, and sharper than any two-edged sword, piercing even to the division of soul and spirit, and of joints and marrow, and is a discerner of the thoughts and intents of the heart." (Heb 4:12).

The greatest evidence that the Bible is The Word of God, is its power to change lives. John Meldau states: "Marcus Aurelius, Confucius and other philosophers wrote some good moral and ethical maxims, but no one is won to a life of holiness by reading them. They present an ideal, but lack the vital power that the Bible alone has to lift the soul to that ideal. The Bible accomplishes this by leading us to direct contact with God, by faith in the Lord Jesus Christ." The Bible's answer to the needs of man is spiritual regeneration, which takes place when an individual acknowledges personal sin and expresses faith in the sacrifice of Christ for that sin. This yields new life and fellowship with the living God – the power of change.

Personal Notes

Psalm 19:1-6

The heavens declare the glory of God; And the firmament shows His handiwork. Day unto day utters speech, And night unto night reveals knowledge. There is no speech nor language Where their voice is not heard. Their line has gone out through all the earth, And their words to the end of the world. In them He has set a tabernacle for the sun, Which is like a bridegroom coming out of his chamber, And rejoices like a strong man to run its race. Its rising is from one end of heaven, And its circuit to the other end; And there is nothing hidden from its heat.

Finding God

An agnostic is someone who hasn't made their mind up about God, an atheist affirms that there is no God. The Bible says the heavens declare the glory of God and the earth shows his handiwork. Can anyone with a truly honest heart look through a microscope at the intricacies of our micro world or look through a telescope at the uniqueness of our mega universe and say there is no designer?

Whenever I come across someone who is unsure of the existence of God I'm inclined to ask: "Have you ever experienced a time when your mind and heart were prompted to acknowledge the presence of God? Has there ever been a time when in the midst of a lightning storm and the demonstration of limitless power, you were prompted to acknowledge God? Have you ever stood, overlooking a scene of nature beautiful enough to take your breath away, and been pressed to acknowledge the artist-Creator?"

Scripture states that God sends Angels as ministering spirits to render service for the sake of those who will inherit salvation (Hebrews 1:14). To the sceptic I'm inclined to ask: "Has there ever been a time in which your destruction seemed imminent, when you sensed a supernatural and providing protection?"

George Macdonald said: "God hides nothing. His very work from the beginning is revelation-a casting aside of veil after veil, a showing unto men of truth after truth. On and on from fact divine he advances, until at length in his Son Jesus he unveils his very face." The evidence of God is everywhere to be found. He does exist, and the honest heart will acknowledge Him. Yet, to know that He exists and fail to know Him is agony to the soul. Knowing Him personally begins with accepting His Son Jesus Christ as our Saviour-access. Jesus said, "I am the way and the truth and the life. No one comes to the Father except through me. I tell you the truth, whoever hears my word and believes him who sent me has eternal life and will not be condemned; he has crossed over from death to life."

During World War II the famous American pilot, Captain Eddie Rickenbacker, was flying on a special mission to the Pacific Islands. The plane crashed, and Rickenbacker and his crew were lost at sea for twenty-one days. Rickenbacker wrote of that experience: "In the beginning many of the men were atheists or agnostics, but at the end of the terrible ordeal each, in his own way, discovered God. Each man found God in the vast, empty loneliness of the ocean. Each man found salvation and strength in prayer, and a community of feeling developed which created a liveliness of human fellowship and worship, and a sense of gentle peace."

Although it may come to a life or death situation to turn a heat toward God, it need not. He evidences His existence everywhere we look. Friend, have you found the living God?

Personal Notes

1 Peter 1:3-26

Blessed be the God and Father of our Lord Jesus Christ, who according to His abundant mercy has begotten us again to a living hope through the resurrection of Jesus Christ from the dead, to an inheritance incorruptible and undefiled and that does not fade away, reserved in heaven for you, who are kept by the power of God through faith for salvation ready to be revealed in the last time. In this you greatly rejoice, though now for a little while, if need be, you have been grieved by various trials, that the genuineness of your faith, being much more precious than gold that perishes, though it is tested by fire, may be found to praise, honor, and glory at the revelation of Jesus Christ, whom having not seen you love. Though now you do not see Him, yet believing, you rejoice with joy inexpressible and full of glory, receiving the end of your faith—the salvation of your souls.

Of this salvation the prophets have inquired and searched carefully, who prophesied of the grace that would come to you, searching what, or what manner of time, the Spirit of Christ who was in them was indicating when He testified beforehand the sufferings of Christ and the glories that would follow. To them it was revealed that, not to themselves, but to us they were ministering the things which now have been reported to you through those who have preached the gospel to you by the Holy Spirit sent from heaven— things which angels desire to look into. Therefore gird up the loins of your mind, be sober, and rest your hope fully upon the grace that is to be brought to you at the revelation of Jesus Christ; as obedient children, not conforming yourselves to the former lusts, as in your ignorance; but as He who called you is holy, you also be holy in all your conduct, because it is written, "Be holy, for I am holy."

Good Focus

It was the fog-shrouded morning of July 4, 1952 when Florence Chadwick waded into the water off Catalina Island with every intention of swimming the channel to the California coast. Having previously become the first woman to swim the English channel in both directions, all seemed routine. After fifteen hours of strenuous labour in frigid, shark-infested waters, Florence asked to be taken out of the water. Her trainer tried to encourage her to continue believing they were very close to success even though the fog was too thick to see any distance ahead. Florence refused to go on.

Scripture says: "Hope deferred makes the heart sick" (Proverbs 13:12 NIV). Hope delayed or darkened from view only brings defeat; this is certainly true in the life of a Christian. For this reason Peter challenges the believer to avoid that which displaces hope; 1 Peter 1:13 states: "gird up the loins of your mind, be sober, and hope to the end for the grace that is to be brought unto you at the revelation of Jesus Christ."

In the day that Peter wrote, ankle-length items of clothing (tunics and mantles) were the norm. When work in the fields or market, or taking a journey, was undertaken, in order to be unimpeded in movement the hem of these items was drawn between the legs and tucked into the belt (girdle). The word used to describe this practice was "anazonnumi", meaning "gird up". This is the very word Peter uses in this passage to help the believer understand the importance of keeping the mind unimpeded.

Hope can be clouded by allowing the mind to drift. Mental drifting displaces hope by leaving loose ends to trip us, the loose ends of worry and indecision. Even mental laziness is a loose end that takes away hope. When the mind settles with being perpetually spoon-fed or entertained by the thoughts and values of others, rather than thinking through and discovering truth personally, hope remains unplanted in the mind and heart.

God desires His own children to develop the discipline of good mental focus. For this reason, He describes personal enrichment through study of scripture as a labour: "Do your best to present yourself to God as one approved, a workman who does not need to be ashamed and who correctly handles the word of truth." (2 Timothy 2:15 NIV).

Florence Chadwick quit within one half mile of successfully completing her goal. She lost hope because she could not see the goal, hidden by fog. A similar fog can overtake the Christian who will not practice good mental focus, who will not live daily in the light of the promises of God; His care, His comfort, His coming. There is great reward for the believer who, by avoiding mental drifting, refuses to let hope become clouded: "Hope deferred makes the heart sick, but a longing fulfilled is a tree of life" (Proverbs 13:12 NIV).

Personal Notes

Proverbs 16:1-9

The preparations of the heart belong to man, But the answer of the tongue is from the LORD. All the ways of a man are pure in his own eyes, But the LORD weighs the spirits. Commit your works to the LORD, And your thoughts will be established. The LORD has made all for Himself, Yes, even the wicked for the day of doom. Everyone proud in heart is an abomination to the LORD; Though they join forces, none will go unpunished. In mercy and truth Atonement is provided for iniquity; And by the fear of the LORD one departs from evil. When a man's ways please the LORD, He makes even his enemies to be at peace with him. Better is a little with righteousness, Than vast revenues without justice. A man's heart plans his way, But the LORD directs his steps.

God's Guidance

A man asked: "What's the fastest way to get to Toronto?" He was asked "Are you traveling by car or by boat?" "By car." he replied. "That's the fastest way" he was told.

Isn't life just like that? You look for direction and find meaningless advice! Today, more people are looking to tea leaves, palm readers and supposed psychic mentors than ever before. For the Christian, life has divine direction, as Gregory Asimakoupoulos describes: "A certain harbour in Italy can be reached only by sailing up a narrow channel between dangerous rocks and shoals. Over the years, many ships have been wrecked, and navigation is hazardous. To guide the ships safely into port, three lights have been mounted on three huge poles in the harbour. When the three lights are perfectly lined up and seen as one, the ship can safely proceed up the narrow channel. If the pilot sees two or three lights, he knows he's off course and in danger."

God has also provided three beacons to guide us. The same rules of navigation apply--the three lights must be lined up before it is safe for us to proceed. The three harbour lights of guidance are: 1. The Word of God (objective standard) 2. The Holy Spirit (subjective witness) 3. Circumstances (divine providence). Together they assure us that the directions we've received are from God and will lead us safely along his way." (See Psalm 119:105 and Isaiah 30:21).

Does this mean that the person who has accepted Christ as personal Saviour always knows exactly where God is leading? The answer is a definite "yes and no." "Yes", because if a Believer is yielded fully to the Will of God, there will be a confident "Yes, God will lead me

to exactly where He wants me, and that will be the best place for me."
(Romans 8:28 – "All things work together for good to those who love
God"). "No", because sometimes a Believer is called to follow by faith,
one step at a time, and trust God to guide in unknown paths. (Hebrews
11:8 –"By faith Abraham, when he was called to go out into a place
which he should after receive for an inheritance, obeyed; and he went
out, not knowing whither he went").

God gives His children a simple formula for following His
"three lights of guidance": "Commit your works to the Lord and your
thoughts will be established… Man plans his way but God directs his
steps" (Proverbs 3:3, 9). The Believer commits to God's will and
purpose in prayer. In so doing, God promises by His Word and His
indwelling Holy Spirit to clarify our thinking. As thoughts are
clarified, a plan takes shape in mind. As the plan is executed in
practice, God promises to fine tune and further clarify direction by His
intervention. God never leaves His own directionless, even if He only
reveals the next step – which may be prayer! Christian friend, do you
know where you are going?

Personal Notes

2 Peter 1:12-21

For this reason I will not be negligent to remind you always of these things, though you know and are established in the present truth. Yes, I think it is right, as long as I am in this tent, to stir you up by reminding you, knowing that shortly I must put off my tent, just as our Lord Jesus Christ showed me. Moreover I will be careful to ensure that you always have a reminder of these things after my decease. For we did not follow cunningly devised fables when we made known to you the power and coming of our Lord Jesus Christ, but were eyewitnesses of His majesty. For He received from God the Father honor and glory when such a voice came to Him from the Excellent Glory: "This is My beloved Son, in whom I am well pleased." And we heard this voice which came from heaven when we were with Him on the holy mountain. And so we have the prophetic word confirmed, which you do well to heed as a light that shines in a dark place, until the day dawns and the morning star rises in your hearts; knowing this first, that no prophecy of Scripture is of any private interpretation, for prophecy never came by the will of man, but holy men of God spoke as they were moved by the Holy Spirit.

Believing The Bible

For many skeptics, believing the Bible would be foolish trust and arrogant belief. Because the Bible has been blamed for everything from American slavery to African apartheid, including Hitler's war on Jews and Bosnian "ethnic cleansing", skeptics are on the rise! Yet nothing could be farther from the truth than these claims of Bible-invoked inhumanity. On the contrary, when taken at simple face value, properly interpreted with common grammatical study and historical context, the Bible proves to be the most remarkable Book ever written, claiming to be authored by God Himself through the agency of holy men: "for prophecy never came by the will of man, but holy men of God spoke as they were moved by the Holy Spirit" (2 Peter 1:21).

For instance, long before science ever discovered it, the Bible taught the countless number of the stars, the immensity of space, the universal law of motion, the refraction of light, that the earth is a sphere, that the heavens follow orbits, that man is made of the same chemical composition as dust. Although not a book of science, its scientific statements are infallible. The reason for these miraculous declarations, thousands of years before science discovered them, is clear: God, the creator of the universe, is the author of the Bible. Such great men as Lord

Bacon, Professor Gladstone, and French scientist Pasteur accepted the divine authorship of the Bible.

From a moral standpoint, the Bible honestly portrays man as fallen from grace, filled with self-importance, and moved with rebellious revolt against God. Scripture reveals the result of this state: human degradation and self-destruction and man standing in judgment of God even though he chooses to deny God's existence (see Romans 1:18 – 3:20). These statements are as infallible as the Bible's scientific observations and, more importantly, prick the conscience of men: "For the word of God is living and active. Sharper than any double-edged sword, it penetrates even to dividing soul and spirit, joints and marrow; it judges the thoughts and attitudes of the heart" (Hebrews 4:12).

Countless numbers have been stirred to believe the accuracy of the Bible and accept God's stated escape from human degradation. Understanding the intent of God's Word to reveal the sinful nature of man, not for the purpose of promoting it, but for the purpose of remedying it, they have acknowledged the historical accuracy of the claims and ministry of Jesus Christ, and yielded to His saving grace: "For God so loved the world that He gave His only begotten Son, that whoever believes in Him should not perish but have everlasting life. "For God did not send His Son into the world to condemn the world, but that the world through Him might be saved. He who believes in Him is not condemned; but he who does not believe is condemned already, because he has not believed in the name of the only begotten Son of God." (John 3:16-18). Have you considered the implications of the Bible record?

Personal Notes

Romans 1:13-23

Now I do not want you to be unaware, brethren, that I often planned to come to you (but was hindered until now), that I might have some fruit among you also, just as among the other Gentiles. I am a debtor both to Greeks and to barbarians, both to wise and to unwise. So, as much as is in me, I am ready to preach the gospel to you who are in Rome also. For I am not ashamed of the gospel of Christ, for it is the power of God to salvation for everyone who believes, for the Jew first and also for the Greek. For in it the righteousness of God is revealed from faith to faith; as it is written, "The just shall live by faith." For the wrath of God is revealed from heaven against all ungodliness and unrighteousness of men, who suppress the truth in unrighteousness, because what may be known of God is manifest in them, for God has shown it to them. For since the creation of the world His invisible attributes are clearly seen, being understood by the things that are made, even His eternal power and Godhead, so that they are without excuse, because, although they knew God, they did not glorify Him as God, nor were thankful, but became futile in their thoughts, and their foolish hearts were darkened. Professing to be wise, they became fools, and changed the glory of the incorruptible God into an image made like corruptible man—and birds and four-footed animals and creeping things.

Believing Creation

"In the beginning God created the heavens and the earth." These first words of Scripture, when taken literally, offer an explanation for the origin of the universe and all it contains, "making no apology for the fact that the account involves supernatural creation *ex nihilo*, creation of something from nothing." It is this clear claim of supernatural creation that prompts many today to doubt the integrity of the Bible, due to the wide acceptance of evolutionary theory. "Evolution is not now confined to biological evolution, to which Darwin's name is attached, but has become an ideology that extends onto virtually every area of human activity, including politics." (Quotes: Ian Taylor, "In The Minds of Men: Darwin and the New World Order").

The general public has been kept from the fact that there are gaping holes in the theory of evolution. Attempts to plug these holes have been repeatedly made by scientists in re-defining and reinterpreting the scientific evidence. For instance, in order for evolutionary theory to stand, the earth age must be in excess of billions of years, yet so many observable facts deny this possibility. Scientists know that the sun's constant source of energy is in conflict with old-earth theory. At first this was explained by "sun contraction" under its own gravitation. When this proved to support a young earth, the theory was dropped for a nuclear fusion theory. However, in view of the fact that billions of years of sun's nuclear fusion would bath the earth in subatomic particles called neutrinos, and that there is no evidence of these particles, this theory also was abandoned. The rotation of the sun and the earth, comet age, missing radiogenic helium, stalagmite and stalactite formation, oil well pressure, and even earth population growth, all point to a very young earth. These points are only a small representation of "holes" in one area of evolutionary theory – "earth age." When other areas such as fossil records, geological formations, species propagation, etc. are examined, more "holes" become evident.

God explained man's inclination to turn away from Him over 2000 years ago: "For since the creation of the world His [God's] invisible attributes are clearly seen, being understood by the things that are made, even His eternal power and Godhead, so that they are without excuse, because although they knew God, they did not glorify Him as God, nor were thankful, but became futile in their thoughts, and their foolish hearts were darkened. Professing to be wise, they became fools, and changed the glory of the incorruptible God into an image made like corruptible man----and birds and four-footed animals and creeping things." (Romans 1:20-23). Man would sooner believe a lie, even when the evidence is against it, than acknowledge the existence of God, because to acknowledge God's existence is to accept accountability. Scripture declares: "It is appointed unto men once to die, and then the judgment" (Hebrews 9:27). The Bible says God created and God will judge, have you considered the implications of this?

Personal Notes

Jeremiah 5:20-31

"Declare this in the house of Jacob And proclaim it in Judah, saying, 'Hear this now, O foolish people, Without understanding, Who have eyes and see not, And who have ears and hear not: Do you not fear Me?' says the LORD. 'Will you not tremble at My presence, Who have placed the sand as the bound of the sea, By a perpetual decree, that it cannot pass beyond it? And though its waves toss to and fro, Yet they cannot prevail; Though they roar, yet they cannot pass over it. But this people has a defiant and rebellious heart; They have revolted and departed. They do not say in their heart, "Let us now fear the LORD our God, Who gives rain, both the former and the latter, in its season. He reserves for us the appointed weeks of the harvest." Your iniquities have turned these things away, And your sins have withheld good from you. 'For among My people are found wicked men; They lie in wait as one who sets snares; They set a trap; They catch men. As a cage is full of birds, So their houses are full of deceit. Therefore they have become great and grown rich. They have grown fat, they are sleek; Yes, they surpass the deeds of the wicked; They do not plead the cause, The cause of the fatherless; Yet they prosper, And the right of the needy they do not defend. Shall I not punish them for these things?' says the LORD. 'Shall I not avenge Myself on such a nation as this?' "An astonishing and horrible thing Has been committed in the land: The prophets prophesy falsely, And the priests rule by their own power; And My people love to have it so. But what will you do in the end?

Odds or Evens?

Dr. Jerome Frank told this story: "… a man I was sitting next to on a coast-to-coast flight told me, "You know, I used to be deathly afraid of flying. It all started after that man brought a bomb on board a flight to Denver to kill his mother-in-law. I could never get it out of my mind that someone on board one of my flights might also be carrying a bomb."

I asked, "Well, what did you do about it?"

He replied, "Well, I went to one of those special schools for people who are afraid of flying and they told me there was only one chance in ten thousand that someone would be on board my flight with a bomb. That didn't make me feel much better. The odds were still too close. But then I reasoned that if there was only one chance in ten thousand that one bomb would be on the plane, there was only one chance in 100 million that two bombs would be on board. And I could live with those odds."

So I asked, "But what good would that do you?"

He quickly replied, "Ever since then, I carry one bomb on board myself--just to improve the odds."

Few would consider this attempt at improving the odds a sensible choice, yet too many people approach eternity in the same manner. Often when I ask whether a person believes he or she will spend eternity in heaven with God the response is: "Well, I've tried to live the best I can and I think the good I've done will out-weigh any sin I've committed!" God never made the assurance of heaven an attempt to better the odds. As a matter of fact, heaven has nothing to do with "the best I can do" or with "the good I've done."

Scripture removes that philosophical approach. "At one time we too were foolish, disobedient, deceived and enslaved by all kinds of passions and pleasures... But when the kindness and love of God our Saviour appeared, he saved us, not because of righteous things we had done, but because of his mercy. He saved us through the washing of rebirth and renewal by the Holy Spirit, whom he poured out on us generously through Jesus Christ our Saviour, so that, having been justified by his grace, we might become heirs having the hope of eternal life." (Titus 3:3-7).

God makes the assurance of heaven a matter of *belief* in the mercy of Christ's sacrifice on Calvary to pay the penalty of our sin, and *faith* in the power of Christ's resurrection to implant new life into a believer by the presence of the Holy Spirit. It is God's work for us that provides forgiveness and God's work in us that transforms the heart. Being saved from eternal loss is to be forgiven alone, doing good is the result of the transformation of salvation whereby a believer seeks to honour God in all things. Friend, you don't have to play the odds, God already evened the score, just believe!

Personal Notes

John 19:23-27

Then the soldiers, when they had crucified Jesus, took His garments and made four parts, to each soldier a part, and also the tunic. Now the tunic was without seam, woven from the top in one piece. They said therefore among themselves, "Let us not tear it, but cast lots for it, whose it shall be," that the Scripture might be fulfilled which says: "They divided My garments among them, And for My clothing they cast lots." Therefore the soldiers did these things. Now there stood by the cross of Jesus His mother, and His mother's sister, Mary the wife of Clopas, and Mary Magdalene. When Jesus therefore saw His mother, and the disciple whom He loved standing by, He said to His mother, "Woman, behold your son!" Then He said to the disciple, "Behold your mother!" And from that hour that disciple took her to his own home.

Jesus Honours Motherhood from the Cross

If during a Christian marriage ceremony we are reminded of Christ's sanctioning marriage by his presence at the wedding of Cana, how much more are we reminded of Christ's honouring of motherhood when, upon the cross of Calvary as He bore the sin of the whole world, Jesus acknowledged his own mother's needs. "Now there stood by the cross of Jesus His mother, and His mother's sister, Mary the wife of Clopas, and Mary Magdalene. When Jesus therefore saw His mother, and the disciple whom He loved standing by, He said to His mother, "Woman, behold your son!" Then He said to the disciple, "Behold your mother!" And from that hour that disciple took her to his own home." (John 19:25-27).

J. Oswald Sanders in *The Incomparable Christ* addresses the significance of this text with these thoughts: "Our Lord left an example for all whose parents are still living. He honoured His mother. The growing disregard on the part of young people of their obligations to parents is fraught with serious social consequences. All obligation to parents does not cease when children become of age; it is true they are no longer under parental control, but that does not absolve them from the necessity of continuing to honour father and mother... There is no excuse that is valid before God for neglecting one's parents, and if there has been such neglect, the path of blessing will be to make amends at once... He [Jesus] demonstrated that the fact of our having responsibilities in spiritual work does not relieve us of our natural obligations... Holiness never thrives on neglected duties."

James Dobson wrote: "Countless times each day a mother does what no one else can do quite as well. She wipes away a tear, whispers a word of hope, eases a child's fear. She teaches, ministers, loves, and nurtures the next generation of citizens. And she challenges and cajoles her kids to do their best and be the best. But no editorials praise these accomplishments-where is the coverage our mothers rightfully deserve?"

We might well have excused Jesus, had he been so occupied with the great work of redemption, providing an avenue of forgiveness for a world by his own substitution death, that He overlooked His own mother's needs. But such was not the case. In tender love, though the weight of the whole world was upon His shoulders, He ministered tenderly, almost as a last will and testament, to His mother's needs. Christian friend, does the love of Christ so abide in His own children's hearts, or has the busyness of life and distractions of routine kept our mothers in the background of our thoughts and time?

"Thank you, God,
For pretending not to notice that one of
Your angels is missing and for guiding her to me.
You must have known how much I would need her, so
You turned your head for a minute and allowed her
to slip away to me.
Sometimes I wonder what special name you had for her.
I call her "Mother."   Bernice Maddux

Personal Notes

Genesis 4:3-15

And in the process of time it came to pass that Cain brought an offering of the fruit of the ground to the LORD. Abel also brought of the firstborn of his flock and of their fat. And the LORD respected Abel and his offering, but He did not respect Cain and his offering. And Cain was very angry, and his countenance fell. So the LORD said to Cain, "Why are you angry? And why has your countenance fallen? "If you do well, will you not be accepted? And if you do not do well, sin lies at the door. And its desire is for you, but you should rule over it." Now Cain talked with Abel his brother; and it came to pass, when they were in the field, that Cain rose up against Abel his brother and killed him. Then the LORD said to Cain, "Where is Abel your brother?" He said, "I do not know. Am I my brother's keeper?" And He said, "What have you done? The voice of your brother's blood cries out to Me from the ground. "So now you are cursed from the earth, which has opened its mouth to receive your brother's blood from your hand. "When you till the ground, it shall no longer yield its strength to you. A fugitive and a vagabond you shall be on the earth." And Cain said to the LORD, "My punishment is greater than I can bear! "Surely You have driven me out this day from the face of the ground; I shall be hidden from Your face; I shall be a fugitive and a vagabond on the earth, and it will happen that anyone who finds me will kill me." And the LORD said to him, "Therefore, whoever kills Cain, vengeance shall be taken on him sevenfold." And the LORD set a mark on Cain, lest anyone finding him should kill him.

Avoiding the Agents of Destruction

Philip Yancey wrote: "I have a friend whose marriage has gone through rough times. One night George passed a breaking point and emotionally exploded. He pounded the table and floor. "I hate you!" he screamed at his wife. "I won't take it anymore! I've had enough! I won't go on! I won't let it happen! No! No! No!"

Several months later my friend woke up in the middle of the night and heard strange sounds coming from the room where his 2-year-old son slept. He went down the hall, stood outside his son's door, and shivers ran through his flesh. In a soft voice, the 2-year-old was repeating word for word with precise inflection the climactic argument between his mother and father. "I hate you ... I won't take it anymore ... No! No! No!"

George realized that in some awful way he had just passed on his pain and anger and unforgiveness to the next generation. ... Apart from forgiveness, the monstrous past may awake at any time from hibernation and devour the present--and even the future."

Scripture repeatedly addresses the danger and damage of anger and loose lips: "Cease from anger, and forsake wrath; Do not fret--it only causes harm." (Psalm 37:8) , "So then, my beloved brethren, let every man be swift to hear, slow to speak, slow to wrath; for the wrath of man does not produce the righteousness of God." (James 1:19-20). God offers a replacement program for the anger mentioned in Psalm 37 where "to fret" means to become hot or furious with anger. To those who have put their trust in Christ as Saviour, when the temptation to anger arises, God suggests a seven step procedure in Psalm 37:

Step 1 - Trust in the LORD (have confidence in God), Step 2 - Do good (be pleasant and agreeable in order to minister to others), Step 3 - Dwell in the land (or make yourself at home with God in whatever circumstances you find yourself). Step 4 - Feed on His faithfulness (let God shepherd you by His Promises). Step 5 - Delight yourself also in the LORD (be happy about God's tender loving care). Step 6 - Commit your way to the LORD (turn all your paths and purposes over to God). Step 7 – Return to the first step -Trust also in Him (Psalm 37:3-5).

And what is the reward of disciplining oneself to these steps of fellowship? God's special promises: "But the meek shall inherit the earth, And shall delight themselves in the abundance of peace." (Psalm 37:11). These steps secure a cycle of deepening relationship to God. Like the giving of a ring in marriage to symbolize unbroken love, this cycle guarantees unbroken fellowship and affords the believer with peace to overcome anger. Christian friend, don't let anger and the loose tongue be agents of destruction in your life, follow God's steps of fellowship and let His peace rule your heart.

Personal Notes

Psalm 63:1-11

O God, You are my God; Early will I seek You; My soul thirsts for You; My flesh longs for You In a dry and thirsty land Where there is no water. So I have looked for You in the sanctuary, To see Your power and Your glory. Because Your lovingkindness is better than life, My lips shall praise You. Thus I will bless You while I live; I will lift up my hands in Your name. My soul shall be satisfied as with marrow and fatness, And my mouth shall praise You with joyful lips. When I remember You on my bed, I meditate on You in the night watches. Because You have been my help, Therefore in the shadow of Your wings I will rejoice. My soul follows close behind You; Your right hand upholds me. But those who seek my life, to destroy it, Shall go into the lower parts of the earth. They shall fall by the sword; They shall be a portion for jackals. But the king shall rejoice in God; Everyone who swears by Him shall glory; But the mouth of those who speak lies shall be stopped.

Relaxation by Contemplation.

Andrew Greeley made this statement: "Contemplation is a casualty of the America way of life. We simply don't have time for it ... our nation has so much leisure time that it has a leisure problem, and yet it lacks the essential leisure of contemplation." For the Christian, such a careless use of time is inexcusable, for God delights to occupy the mind and heart of His own children. Taking time to explore the depths of God through meaningful contemplation of His Word is a rewarding adventure.

Consider the joy the Psalmist found when turning his thoughts toward the Messiah: "My heart is overflowing with a good theme; I recite my composition concerning the King; My tongue is the pen of a ready writer. You are fairer than the sons of men; Grace is poured upon Your lips; Therefore God has blessed You forever. Gird Your sword upon Your thigh, O Mighty One, With Your glory and Your majesty. And in Your majesty ride prosperously because of truth, humility, and righteousness... Your throne, O God, is forever and ever; A scepter of righteousness is the scepter of Your kingdom. You love righteousness and hate wickedness; Therefore God, Your God, has anointed You With the oil of gladness more than Your companions." (from Psalm 45).

When the Psalmist allowed his mind and heart to feed on thoughts of the promised Messiah-King (the original Hebrew word translated "overflowing" suggests the benefits of a process of digestion), his tongue could not keep silent. He was awe struck at the beauty, grace, and righteous character of God's appointed sovereign. The result was "A Song of Loves" written to be played on the stringed instrument called a "Shoshannim" for the sons of Korah to sing in praise of God.

Jesus stated that "Man shall not live by bread alone but by every word that proceeds out of the mouth of God" (Matt. 4:4). With these words, He addressed more than mere obedience, He made reference to the very essence of spiritual life, found by faith in Christ and nurtured by meditation upon God as revealed uniquely in Scripture. To this end the Christian is urged to be renewed in mind and refreshed in spirit through quiet contemplation and personal fellowship with God. This goes beyond meditation, this involves communication with the living God who speaks to man through His Holy Word.

"Flee for a little while thy occupations; hide thyself for a time from thy disturbing thoughts. Cast aside now thy burdensome cares, and put away thy toilsome business. Yield room for some little time to God, and rest for a little time in him. Enter the inner chamber of thy mind; shut out all thoughts save that of God and such as can aid thee in seeking him. Speak now, my whole heart! Speak now to God, saying, "I seek thy face;thy face, Lord, will I seek." Saint Anselm (C. 1033-1109). Christian friend, take time to commune with your God!

Personal Notes

Luke 1:13-17

But the angel said to him, "Do not be afraid, Zacharias, for your prayer is heard; and your wife Elizabeth will bear you a son, and you shall call his name John. "And you will have joy and gladness, and many will rejoice at his birth. "For he will be great in the sight of the Lord, and shall drink neither wine nor strong drink. He will also be filled with the Holy Spirit, even from his mother's womb. "And he will turn many of the children of Israel to the Lord their God. "He will also go before Him in the spirit and power of Elijah, 'to turn the hearts of the fathers to the children,' and the disobedient to the wisdom of the just, to make ready a people prepared for the Lord."

Dear Dads

In an era when media mocks the integrity of marriage fidelity and society downplays the importance of the family, wisdom calls for a return to the architect of the home for His master plan. Scripture states: "Unless the LORD builds the house, its builders labour in vain." (Psalm 127:1). The father plays a specific and vital role in God's master plan. One of the most important "hats" a Dad is called to wear is the hat of the instructor. "Fathers, do not exasperate your children; instead, bring them up in the training and instruction of the Lord." (Ephesians 6:4 NIV). The "training" referred to is the establishing of Biblical rules and values for the home. It involves setting the boundaries of appropriate behaviour and exercising discipline when the boundaries are exceeded. It involves giving counsel and direction, sharing God's principles, and discussing the reasons, and blessings for choosing God's values.

Here are the thoughts of some godly men on this topic. Billy Graham suggests parents give children "a target to shoot at… a goal to work toward…. a pattern that they can see clearly, and you give them something that gold and silver cannot buy." Charles Haddon Spurgeon put the essence of this "training" to a poem: "Ere a child has reached to seven, Teach him all the way to heaven; Better still the work will thrive, If he learns before he's five."

Johann Heinrich Pestalozzi made this observation: "The best way for a child to learn to fear God is to know a real Christian. The best way for a child to learn to pray is to live with a father and mother who know a life of friendship with God and who truly pray." Charles A. Wells stated, "The school will teach children how to read, but the environment of the home must teach them what to read. The school can teach them how to think, but the home must teach them what to believe." James Dobson suggests: "While yielding to loving parental leadership, children are also learning to yield to the benevolent leadership of God himself."

The father's responsibility of spiritual leadership is vital. The Bible affirms that parents "Train a child in the way he should go, and when he is old he will not turn from it." (Proverbs 6:22). Unfortunately, this principle works negatively as well. "If a child sees his parents day in and day out living without self-restraint or self-discipline, then he will come in the deepest fibers of his being to believe that that is the way to live." (Scott Peck).

It is apparent that the father who successfully fills God's "master plan" of parenting must first know and follow God himself. Jesus said, "He that believeth on me, as the scripture hath said, out of his belly shall flow rivers of living water." (John 7:38). Dear Dads – is your relation to Christ such that He can pour from your life, rivers of living water to your own children?

Could I climb to the highest place in Athens, I would lift my voice and proclaim: "Fellow citizens, why do you turn and scrape every stone to gather wealth, and take so little care of your children to whom one day you must relinquish it all?" (Socrates).

When I was around thirteen and my brother was ten, Father promised to take us to the circus. But at lunch there was a phone call. Some urgent business required his attention downtown. My brother and I braced ourselves for the disappointment. Then we heard him say, "No, I won't be down. It will have to wait." When he came back to the table, Mother smiled and said, "The circus keeps coming back, you know." "I know," said Father, "but childhood doesn't." Arthur Gordon.

Personal Notes

Revelation 21:1-7

Now I saw a new heaven and a new earth, for the first heaven and the first earth had passed away. Also there was no more sea. Then I, John, saw the holy city, New Jerusalem, coming down out of heaven from God, prepared as a bride adorned for her husband. And I heard a loud voice from heaven saying, "Behold, the tabernacle of God is with men, and He will dwell with them, and they shall be His people. God Himself will be with them and be their God. "And God will wipe away every tear from their eyes; there shall be no more death, nor sorrow, nor crying. There shall be no more pain, for the former things have passed away." Then He who sat on the throne said, "Behold, I make all things new." And He said to me, "Write, for these words are true and faithful." And He said to me, "It is done! I am the Alpha and the Omega, the Beginning and the End. I will give of the fountain of the water of life freely to him who thirsts. "He who overcomes shall inherit all things, and I will be his God and he shall be My son.

Turned Inside Out

One of the most profound statements of scripture is found in 2 Corinthians 5:17 which states: 'Therefore if any man be in Christ, he is a new creature: old things are passed away; behold, all things are become new." To be "in Christ" is a point of decision based upon belief in three Bible truths. It is first to believe what God says about the spiritual condition of all people: "All have sinned and come short of the glory of God" (Romans 3:23). This means that all mankind, without exception, fall drastically short of God's Holy perfection and therefore are spiritually separated from Him. The consequence of this state is eternal separation from God. The second truth is to believe what God says about man's ability to do something about this condition of separation. He says, "Not by works of righteousness which we have done, but according to his mercy he saved us" (Titus 3:5). Salvation involves a new creation of a person in the fashion that God created the universe – *ex nihilo*, or – out of nothing. Jesus said, "Blessed are the poor in spirit for theirs is the kingdom of God" (Matt. 5:3). The faith that secures salvation admits that there is nothing of worth to offer God that merits any spiritual gain. Salvation is God alone working His grace in the heart of man which brings us to the third truth to be believed – What God did for helpless man. Out of love, God sent His own Son to die as the only acceptable sacrifice (being perfect God and perfect man) for man's sins: "God demonstrated His love for us in that while we were yet sinners, <u>Christ died for us</u>" (Romans 5:8). Christ's death on the cross satisfied the Holy Wrath of God toward sin and provided the only substitution for man's state of death. This was proved to be so by the resurrection from the dead of Jesus, the one that now offers eternal life to all who will believe.

The faith that embraces these three Bible truths, embraces Christ and is found "in Christ" as a "new creation." Salvation involves <u>all things new</u> in a person's life. Being "in Christ" means that Christ is also in us. God's nature of love, holiness, righteousness and goodness begins to be reproduced as a by-product of God's presence in the life of the believer: "The fruit of the spirit is love, joy, peace, longsuffering, gentleness, goodness, faith, meekness, self-control" (Galatians 5:22). Most Christians only begin to grasp the wonder of the statement "all things are become new" acknowledging that salvation is a new beginning. Yet with Paul's statement to the church of Corinth, God has defined salvation as a total and radical remake of the individual and all that pertains to his or her life. The best remake in life is the remake of salvation, it is a change from the inside out. Friend, have you been turned inside out by faith?

Personal Notes

Isaiah 50:4-10

"The Lord GOD has given Me The tongue of the learned, That I should know how to speak A word in season to him who is weary. He awakens Me morning by morning, He awakens My ear To hear as the learned. The Lord GOD has opened My ear; And I was not rebellious, Nor did I turn away. I gave My back to those who struck Me, And My cheeks to those who plucked out the beard; I did not hide My face from shame and spitting. "For the Lord GOD will help Me; Therefore I will not be disgraced; Therefore I have set My face like a flint, And I know that I will not be ashamed. He is near who justifies Me; Who will contend with Me? Let us stand together. Who is My adversary? Let him come near Me. Surely the Lord GOD will help Me; Who is he who will condemn Me? Indeed they will all grow old like a garment; The moth will eat them up. "Who among you fears the LORD? Who obeys the voice of His Servant? Who walks in darkness And has no light? Let him trust in the name of the LORD And rely upon his God.

Help with the Thorns of Life

Faith in Christ as personal Saviour is a life described by God as "all things new" (1 Corinthians 5:17). With this discovery, however, there is often the mistaken idea that the Christian life is a bed of roses without thorns. This was neither true of the early Christians, the apostles, or even Christ. As J. B. Phillips suggests, "Christ made no promise that those who followed him in his plan of re-establishing life on its proper basic principles would enjoy a special immunity from pain and sorrow-nor did he himself experience such immunity. He did, however, promise enough joy and courage, enough love and confidence in God to enable those who went his way to do far more than survive."

One of the real joys of the Christian experience is finding God to be abundantly sufficient in any troublesome circumstance and any burdensome trial. It was the apostle Paul who pleaded with God to heal him of an infirmity that threatened his ministry. Yet God had something better in mind. After pleading in prayer three times for deliverance, God told Paul "My grace is sufficient for thee: for my strength is made perfect in weakness." (2 Corinthians 12:9). And indeed Paul found this to be so, to such an extent that he could latter declare: "I can do all things through Christ who strengthens me" (Philippians 4:13).

Scripture record is resplendent with the accounts of people who, while in deep trial, found God to be all-sufficient. When Hagar was sent packing with her son, finding herself in the wilderness facing imminent death, she called out to God and He delivered her. When Joseph was betrayed by his brothers and sold into slavery things seemed only downhill from there. Yet God not only restored Joseph, he made him a ruler in Egypt as well.   Merv Rosell points out that "God could have kept Daniel out of the lions' den. . . he could have kept Paul and Silas out of jail.. . . he could have kept the three Hebrew children out of the fiery furnace. . . but God has never promised to keep us out of hard places . . . what he has promised is to go with us through every hard place, and to bring us through victoriously."

Salvation is greater than a promise of heaven, it is coming into relationship with Almighty God, whose name is "The All Sufficient One." It was in the midst of a troublesome time, betrayed by a son and abandoned by a close friend, that David discovered the joy of God's sufficiency and urged all others to "Cast your burden on the LORD, and He shall sustain you; He shall never permit the righteous to be moved." (Psalm 55:22). "It doesn't matter how great the pressure is. What really matters is where the pressure lies--whether it comes between you and God or whether it presses you nearer his heart." (James Hudson Taylor). Is God your sufficiency?

Personal Notes

Romans 4:1-13

What then shall we say that Abraham, our forefather, discovered in this matter? If, in fact, Abraham was justified by works, he had something to boast about—but not before God. What does the Scripture say? "Abraham believed God, and it was credited to him as righteousness." Now when a man works, his wages are not credited to him as a gift, but as an obligation. However, to the man who does not work but trusts God who justifies the wicked, his faith is credited as righteousness. David says the same thing when he speaks of the blessedness of the man to whom God credits righteousness apart from works: "Blessed are they whose transgressions are forgiven, whose sins are covered. Blessed is the man whose sin the Lord will never count against him." Is this blessedness only for the circumcised, or also for the uncircumcised? We have been saying that Abraham's faith was credited to him as righteousness. Under what circumstances was it credited? Was it after he was circumcised, or before? It was not after, but before! And he received the sign of circumcision, a seal of the righteousness that he had by faith while he was still uncircumcised. So then, he is the father of all who believe but have not been circumcised, in order that righteousness might be credited to them. And he is also the father of the circumcised who not only are circumcised but who also walk in the footsteps of the faith that our father Abraham had before he was circumcised. It was not through law that Abraham and his offspring received the promise that he would be heir of the world, but through the righteousness that comes by faith.(NIV).

Celebrating Freedom

In the late summer of 1989 one million people in Latvia, Lithuania, and Estonia linked arms and formed a human chain that was 360 miles long. When the chain was completed, one word was passed along the line. Each one spoke to the next until that one word had been passed along all those 360 miles. The word was "freedom!" Up until September 11, 2001 the July joint celebration of national freedom for Canadians and Americans, held so closely together, was perhaps more a holiday to relax than a celebration to reflect upon. Seeing how vulnerable our own safety and security is should have caused due consideration and invoked meaningful thanksgiving for the freedom we do enjoy. Although unlike some countries who have been in bondage to political regimes, the sense of vulnerability that swept across this continent as a result of the attacks of 9-11 undoubtedly awakened an appreciation of the liberty our countries enjoy. To celebrate freedom, with thoughtful reflection, is wise.

There is another freedom that must also be remembered with sober reflection and thanksgiving. When our Lord Jesus Christ cried from the cross "It is finished," he might as well have said "freedom!" Our freedom from sin, our freedom from ourselves, our freedom from death and the grave were all won on the cross and celebrated in the resurrection. To all who in faith, call upon the Lord, there is found the freedom of eternal life. "The word is near you, in your mouth and in your heart" (that is, the word of faith which we preach). "That if you confess with your mouth the Lord Jesus and believe in your heart that God has raised Him from the dead, you will be saved. For with the heart one believes unto righteousness, and with the mouth confession is made unto salvation." (from Romans 10).

With each of the freedoms mentioned above, national and eternal, there can be an observation from without or participation from within. To enjoy the freedom of our nations, one must enter our borders, to enjoy the freedom of God's salvation, one must also enter in. The one great difference regarding these freedoms is this: due to our own immigration laws, not all are invited to enter into our countries freedom; however, God invites all to enter into His eternal freedom. "Most assuredly, I say to you, he who hears My word and believes in Him who sent Me has everlasting life, and shall not come into judgment, but has passed from death into life(from John 5).

On a wall in the vicarage at Olney, England, clergyman and hymn writer, John Newton, wrote Deuteronomy 15:15 (KJV): "and thou shalt remember that thou wast a bondsman in the land of Egypt, and the Lord thy God redeemed thee." It reminded Newton of his days as a slave trader and then as the slave. It also reminded him of the larger freedom he had found in Jesus Christ. Friend, can you celebrate both national and eternal freedom? Reflect upon it!

Personal Notes

157

Psalm 119:105-112

Thy word is a lamp unto my feet, and a light unto my path. I have sworn, and I will perform it, that I will keep thy righteous judgments. I am afflicted very much: quicken me, O LORD, according unto thy word. Accept, I beseech thee, the freewill offerings of my mouth, O LORD, and teach me thy judgments. My soul is continually in my hand: yet do I not forget thy law. The wicked have laid a snare for me: yet I erred not from thy precepts. Thy testimonies have I taken as an heritage forever: for they are the rejoicing of my heart. I have inclined mine heart to perform thy statutes alway, even unto the end.

God's Light

There was a day in southern Ontario when the smoke from forest fires in Quebec choked out the sun and blanketed the sky with the telltale residue of destruction. It reminded me of the verse in Scripture "Where there is no vision the people perish" (Proverbs 29:18). The word here translated vision means an "oracle," or "prophecy" involving some divine communication. Perhaps a clearer translation would be "Where there is no revelation, the people cast off restraint." However the point is the same-- without spiritual enlightenment from God, man has no hope. The text begs the question "Where are we without God's light?"

Scripture states that God's Word is to be the light of our daily path. "Your word is a lamp to my feet and a light to my path." (Psalm 119:105). By precept and by principle, God's Holy Word, the Bible, is offered as a guide to assure a divinely directed life. This was so important that Jesus stated it in terms of life itself. "Man shall not live by bread alone, but by every Word that proceeds out of the mouth of God" (Matthew 4:4).

According to John 1:1, Jesus himself is the "Word of God that became flesh." In others words, when God's eternal Son, became man through the miracle of the virgin conception, God revealed Himself by a special revelation whereby mankind "beheld His glory, the glory as of the only begotten of the Father, full of grace and truth" (John 1:14). As both God and man, Jesus declared "I am the light of the world: he that follows me shall not walk in darkness, but shall have the light of life." (John 8:12).

However, Jesus also spoke of another light that often turns man's heart away from God's light. "The lamp of the body is the eye.

If therefore your eye is good, your whole body will be full of light. But if your eye is bad, your whole body will be full of darkness. If therefore the light that is in you is darkness, how great is that darkness! No one can serve two masters; for either he will hate the one and love the other, or else he will be loyal to the one and despise the other. You cannot serve God and money." The heart of man is turned by whatever fills his eye. If possessions and pleasures fill the eye, then the darkness of this present world chokes out the light of Christ as a telltale sign of pending judgment.

Jesus spoke of one last light, His light of Christian witness. To His own followers Jesus said: "You are the light of the world. ..."Let your light so shine before men, that they may see your good works and glorify your Father in heaven." (Matthew 5:14,16).

The light of nature, the light of science, the light of reason, are but as darkness compared with the divine light which shines only from God. Do you walk in darkness or in light?

Personal Notes

Psalm 119:105-112

Then Jesus cried out and said, "He who believes in Me, believes not in Me but in Him who sent Me. "And he who sees Me sees Him who sent Me. "I have come as a light into the world, that whoever believes in Me should not abide in darkness. "And if anyone hears My words and does not believe, I do not judge him; for I did not come to judge the world but to save the world. "He who rejects Me, and does not receive My words, has that which judges him—the word that I have spoken will judge him in the last day. "For I have not spoken on My own authority; but the Father who sent Me gave Me a command, what I should say and what I should speak. "And I know that His command is everlasting life. Therefore, whatever I speak, just as the Father has told Me, so I speak."

Losing the Compass

With dishonesty and selfish gain so prominent in the world of "corporate business" that governments have to step in to curb the consequences, the question begs to be asked, "How have we sunk so low?" While psychologists may suggest that social pressures have yielded predictable social vices, and while economists may argue that unavoidable financial fractures have resulted in ethical miscalculations, God has a simpler answer, "For since the creation of the world God's invisible qualities-- his eternal power and divine nature-- have been clearly seen, being understood from what has been made, so that men are without excuse. For although they knew God, they neither glorified him as God nor gave thanks to him, but their thinking became futile and their foolish hearts were darkened. Although they claimed to be wise, they became fools... and worshiped and served created things rather than the Creator " (Romans 1:20-25).

When any society dismisses the evidence of God so clearly seen in creation, (as our society has done through the general acceptance as fact of the theory of evolution), and worships creation rather than the creator, that society loses its moral compass in spiritual darkness! In this darkness man gropes for meaning, scratches out an existence on any conceivable platform of thought that is socially accepted. The result is a society that is willing to trade integrity for pragmatism (the end justifies the means), willing to trade purity for hedonism (if it feels good, do it). The consequences of such platforms of thought are impending collapse of economies as mistrust and uncetainty settle into hearts.

L.S. Walker said: "The world is looking for men who are not for sale, men who are honest, sound from centre to circumstance, true to the heart's core, men with conscience as steady as the needle to the pole; men who will stand for right if the heavens tilt and the earth reels; men who will tell the truth and look the world right in the eye; men who neither drag nor run, men who can have courage without shouting it; men in whom courage of everlasting life runs still, deep and strong; men who know their message and tell it; men who know their place and fill it; men who know their business and attend to it; men who will not lie, shirk, or dodge; men who are not too lazy to work, nor too proud to be poor."

Such men do not rise out of darkness, but blossom from the light of God. Such men have seen the light of God, received the light of God, pursued the light of God and have become lights for God. Jesus said, "I am come a light into the world, that whosoever believeth on me should not abide in darkness" (John 12:4) and "I am the light of the world: he that follows me shall not walk in darkness but shall have the light of life." (John 8:12). Your moral and ethical compass will lead you! Are you groping in darkness or blossoming in God's light?

Personal Notes

John 11:17-27

So when Jesus came, He found that he had already been in the tomb four days. Now Bethany was near Jerusalem, about two miles away. And many of the Jews had joined the women around Martha and Mary, to comfort them concerning their brother. Then Martha, as soon as she heard that Jesus was coming, went and met Him, but Mary was sitting in the house. Then Martha said to Jesus, "Lord, if You had been here, my brother would not have died. "But even now I know that whatever You ask of God, God will give You." Jesus said to her, "Your brother will rise again." Martha said to Him, "I know that he will rise again in the resurrection at the last day." Jesus said to her, "I am the resurrection and the life. He who believes in Me, though he may die, he shall live. "And whoever lives and believes in Me shall never die. Do you believe this?" She said to Him, "Yes, Lord, I believe that You are the Christ, the Son of God, who is to come into the world."

The Sting of Death

At the one-hundredth anniversary celebrations of Christian Missionary labours in Zaire, West Africa a startling revelation took place. An old native insisted that he alone had information to be heard. He said that when missionaries came a hundred years before, his people thought their message unusual. Therefore, the tribal leaders decided to test the missionaries by slowly poisoning them. Over a period of years missionary children died one by one. Yet, he said, it was as we watched how they died, that we decided we wanted this Christian life.

True Christianity, as defined by the Bible declares that death holds no power over the believer. Christ said, "I am the resurrection, and the life: he that believeth in me, though he were dead, yet shall he live." (John 11). Paul declared, "O death, where is thy sting? O grave, where is thy victory? The sting of death is sin; and the strength of sin is the law. But thanks be to God, which giveth us the victory through our Lord Jesus Christ." (1 Corinthians 15).

Death is the separation of man's soul and spirit from the physical body and from the living God. It is the consequence of sin. "Wherefore, as by one man sin entered into the world, and death by sin; and so death passed upon all men, for that all have sinned" (Romans 5:12). Jesus Christ, being perfect man and perfect God, suffered punishment and death as a substitute for man's sin. "For he hath made him to be sin for us, who knew no sin; that we might be made the righteousness of God in Him" (2 Corinthians 5:21). This is the significance of Good Friday.

Death was defeated when Jesus rose from the death, proving His sacrifice to be a sufficient substitution and payment for sin before the righteous Father in heaven: "This Jesus hath God raised up, whereof we all are witnesses. Therefore being by the right hand of God exalted, and having received of the Father the promise of the Holy Ghost" (Acts 2). This is the significance of Easter Sunday.

As individuals turn in repentance from their own sins and efforts of seeking acceptance with God, to trust in the substitution and resurrection of Jesus, God declares them to be righteous by faith and imparts eternal life by the Holy Spirit. "Righteousness... shall be imputed, if we believe on him that raised up Jesus our Lord from the dead; Who was delivered for our offences, and was raised again for our justification." (Romans 4:24-25), "For the wages of sin is death; but the gift of God is eternal life through Jesus Christ our Lord" (Romans 6:23). Death, in terms of the spirit's departure from the body may be the experience of a Christian, but such an experience translates the believer from a of spiritual fellowship with the living God to being in the very presence of God. The "sting" of death is gone! Reader, what hold does death have on you?

Personal Notes

163

Ephesians 2:14-22

For He Himself is our peace, who has made both one, and has broken down the middle wall of separation, having abolished in His flesh the enmity, that is, the law of commandments contained in ordinances, so as to create in Himself one new man from the two, thus making peace, and that He might reconcile them both to God in one body through the cross, thereby putting to death the enmity. And He came and preached peace to you who were afar off and to those who were near. For through Him we both have access by one Spirit to the Father. Now, therefore, you are no longer strangers and foreigners, but fellow citizens with the saints and members of the household of God, having been built on the foundation of the apostles and prophets, Jesus Christ Himself being the chief cornerstone, in whom the whole building, being joined together, grows into a holy temple in the Lord, in whom you also are being built together for a dwelling place of God in the Spirit.

War

"War is an evil thing; but to submit to the dictation of other states is worse. . . . Freedom, if we hold fast to it, will ultimately restore our losses, but submission will mean permanent loss of all that we value." Thucydides (460-C. 401 B.C.) "War is the most ghastly experience that can come to any country. And always it is the people-not the handful of men in positions of power-who must pay the full price. The price in dollars and cents. The price in dismembered families. The price in heart agonies. The price in bodily suffering... Always it is the masses who pay." Robert Marion La Follette (1855-1925), "The tragedy of war is that it uses man's best to do man's worst." Harry Emerson Fosdick (1878-1969).

Whole volumes have been written and countless comments have been made about war, yet only the Bible states clearly its origin: "Where do wars and fights come from among you? Do they not come from your desires for pleasure that war in your members? You lust and do not have. You murder and covet and cannot obtain. You fight and war. Yet you do not have because you do not ask." (James 4:1-2). War is the result of a covetous humanity that has turned its back on God. This covetous characteristic was the result of Adam's fall from grace in disobedience that left mankind with a sin nature focussed on self-interest and separated from God. That separation is the state of spiritual death and certain physical death as a wages of sin (Romans 6:23).

Uniquely, it was another war that gave mankind hope for peace with mankind by ensuring peace with God first. Jesus said, "These things I have spoken to you, that in Me you may have peace. In the world you will have tribulation; but be of good cheer, I have overcome the world." (John 16:33). Jesus was speaking of his arrest and ultimate death upon the cross of Calvary. Although this hour of spiritual warfare would scatter his disciples, he assured them of victory over the plight of the world - the sin that separates man from God. And that battle was won. " For if by the one man's offence [Adam's] death reigned through the one, much more those who receive abundance of grace and of the gift of righteousness will reign in life through the One, Jesus Christ. Therefore, as through one man's offence judgment came to all men, resulting in condemnation, even so through one Man's righteous act the free gift came to all men, resulting in justification of life." (Romans 5:17-18), "For He [God] made Him [Jesus] who knew no sin to be sin for us, that we might become the righteousness of God in Him." (2 Corinthians 5:21) , "that if you confess with your mouth the Lord Jesus and believe in your heart that God has raised Him from the dead, you will be saved. " (Romans 10:9). Have you accepted Christ's provision of peace?

Personal Notes

Matthew 5:3-16

"Blessed are the poor in spirit, For theirs is the kingdom of heaven. Blessed are those who mourn, For they shall be comforted. Blessed are the meek, For they shall inherit the earth. Blessed are those who hunger and thirst for righteousness, For they shall be filled. Blessed are the merciful, For they shall obtain mercy. Blessed are the pure in heart, For they shall see God. Blessed are the peacemakers, For they shall be called sons of God. Blessed are those who are persecuted for righteousness' sake, For theirs is the kingdom of heaven. "Blessed are you when they revile and persecute you, and say all kinds of evil against you falsely for My sake. "Rejoice and be exceedingly glad, for great is your reward in heaven, for so they persecuted the prophets who were before you.

"You are the salt of the earth; but if the salt loses its flavor, how shall it be seasoned? It is then good for nothing but to be thrown out and trampled underfoot by men. "You are the light of the world. A city that is set on a hill cannot be hidden. "Nor do they light a lamp and put it under a basket, but on a lampstand, and it gives light to all who are in the house. "Let your light so shine before men, that they may see your good works and glorify your Father in heaven.

Christmas Lights All Year Round

Now that the beautiful blanket of snow has either disappeared or faded to dirty slush in most areas, Christmas time outdoor lights will also disappear. Such seasonal lights are an example of what Christians are to be the whole year round. In contrast to an unbelieving world, the "life direction or path" of all who have accepted Christ as personal Saviour is to be an expanding light: "the path of the just is like the shining sun, that shines ever brighter unto the perfect day. The way of the wicked is like darkness; They do not know what makes them stumble." (Proverbs 4:18-19). In his commentary on Proverbs, Charles Bridges suggests that this verse "rebukes a static profession, a backslidden state… Christian living must be a shining, progressive light." God intended the very life pattern of His children to be as distinct from the unbelieving crowd as the sun's brightness is from darkness.

To His followers Jesus said, "You are the light of the world. A city that is set on a hill cannot be hidden. Nor do they light a lamp and put it under a basket, but on a lampstand, and it gives light to all who are in the house. Let your light so shine before men, that they may see your good works and glorify your Father in heaven." (Matt. 5:14-16). Christians are to be a directing light, where the activity of believers is viewed by the unbelieving world as good works, benevolent endeavors and loving care. Such activity or deeds point to the nature of the God in whom Christians trust so that He receives all the praise and glory.

Paul challenged the believers to understand the transforming nature of their lives as enriching lights: "But we all, with unveiled face, beholding as in a mirror the glory of the Lord, are being transformed into the same image from glory to glory, just as by the Spirit of the Lord." (2 Corinthians 3:18). As the indwelling Spirit of God is given full reign in a believer's life, God develops Christ-like character in that life. It is compared to the "holy glow" on the face of Moses because he spent time in the very presence of God. This transformation is described as the fruit of the Spirit. "But the fruit of the Spirit is love, joy, peace, longsuffering, kindness, goodness, faithfulness, gentleness, self-control." (Galatians 5:22).

Now colourful outdoor lights appear, setting our communities aglow, announcing the season of Christmas. At the first Christmas, a star appeared to announce the coming of the Saviour. God intends light to announce His Son. In life direction, in meaningful deeds, and in character transformation, Christians are God's light to set a world aglow and announce "Jesus is the Son of God, Saviour of the world... and the one who set my heart aglow with His gift of eternal life!" Have you followed God's light to His Son? Are you a responsible light for His Son? Christian friend, light up your world!

Personal Notes

1 Peter 1:1-9

Peter, an apostle of Jesus Christ, To the pilgrims of the Dispersion in Pontus, Galatia, Cappadocia, Asia, and Bithynia, elect according to the foreknowledge of God the Father, in sanctification of the Spirit, for obedience and sprinkling of the blood of Jesus Christ: Grace to you and peace be multiplied. Blessed be the God and Father of our Lord Jesus Christ, who according to His abundant mercy has begotten us again to a living hope through the resurrection of Jesus Christ from the dead, to an inheritance incorruptible and undefiled and that does not fade away, reserved in heaven for you, who are kept by the power of God through faith for salvation ready to be revealed in the last time. In this you greatly rejoice, though now for a little while, if need be, you have been grieved by various trials, that the genuineness of your faith, being much more precious than gold that perishes, though it is tested by fire, may be found to praise, honour, and glory at the revelation of Jesus Christ, whom having not seen you love. Though now you do not see Him, yet believing, you rejoice with joy inexpressible and full of glory, receiving the end of your faith—the salvation of your souls.

Faith's Eye Opener

A Soviet encyclopaedia offers this definition of God: "A mythically invented personality. Progressive materialism and scientific opinion cannot be reconciled with faith in God." This definition has one true element, knowledge of God does requires faith! This is not a faith that assumes the existence of God and then lives out the faith in a manner equivalent to "the power of positive thinking." No, this is a faith that opens the eyes of understanding and secures a real relationship with the living God.

Here is what Scripture says about this faith: "Now faith is the substance of things hoped for, the evidence of things not seen. For by it the elders obtained a good testimony. By faith we understand that the worlds were framed by the word of God, so that the things which are seen were not made of things which are visible… But without faith it is impossible to please Him, for he who comes to God must believe that He is, and that He is a rewarder of those who diligently seek Him." Faith is here *defined* as the solid ground (substance) that hope stands upon. Faith is *described* as the test of proof (evidence) of unseen things. Faith here *acquires* a "well done" from God himself, who is pleased with the exercise of faith in His Word, in the absence of His visible presence. All this is so because faith's *vision* sees the world from God's viewpoint as creator, and sees God's promises as real as earth itself: "These all died in faith, not having received the promises, but having seen them afar off were assured of them, embraced them and confessed that they were strangers and pilgrims on the earth… But now they desire a better, that is, a heavenly country. Therefore, God is not ashamed to be called their God, for He has prepared a city for them." (Heb. 11) Here, faith's *confession* of "we are strangers" embraces all of life (its values, its ethics, its goals, its priorities), within the context of belonging to God. He in turn, brings His own assurance in their heart's that He is their God, by His indwelling Spirit: "The Spirit Himself bears witness with our spirit that we are children of God" (Romans 8:16).

This "faith that opens the eyes of understanding and secures a real relationship with the living God" is so unique that God speaks of the occasion of this faith in terms of rebirth. "Jesus answered, "Most assuredly, I say to you, unless one is born of water and the Spirit, he cannot enter the kingdom of God. "That which is born of the flesh is flesh, and that which is born of the Spirit is spirit… The wind blows where it wishes, and you hear the sound of it, but cannot tell where it comes from and where it goes. So is everyone who is born of the Spirit… For God so loved the world that He gave His only begotten Son, that whoever believes [exercises faith] in Him should not perish but have everlasting life." (John 3:5-8, 16) Have you a seeing faith?

Personal Notes

Deuteronomy 4:14-20

"And the LORD commanded me at that time to teach you statutes and judgments, that you might observe them in the land which you cross over to possess. "Take careful heed to yourselves, for you saw no form when the LORD spoke to you at Horeb out of the midst of the fire, "lest you act corruptly and make for yourselves a carved image in the form of any figure: the likeness of male or female, "the likeness of any animal that is on the earth or the likeness of any winged bird that flies in the air, "the likeness of anything that creeps on the ground or the likeness of any fish that is in the water beneath the earth. "And take heed, lest you lift your eyes to heaven, and when you see the sun, the moon, and the stars, all the host of heaven, you feel driven to worship them and serve them, which the LORD your God has given to all the peoples under the whole heaven as a heritage. "But the LORD has taken you and brought you out of the iron furnace, out of Egypt, to be His people, an inheritance, as you are this day.

Removing God

When modern, educated man voted to remove God from the textbooks of our nation, moral and ethical restraint was unplugged and society was sent in a spiral decent down the drain to the sewers of corruption. These may be strong words of pessimism, nevertheless, our world is evidencing daily the consequences of forgetting about God.

Our nation is looking more and more like that described by Paul, "And even as they did not like to retain God in [their] knowledge, God gave them over to a debased mind, to do those things which are not fitting; Being filled with all unrighteousness, sexual immorality, wickedness, covetousness, maliciousness; full of envy, murder, strife, deceit, evil-mindedness; they are whisperers, backbiters, haters of God, violent, proud, boasters, inventors of evil things, disobedient to parents, undiscerning, untrustworthy, unloving, unforgiving, unmerciful:" (Romans 1:28-31).

The sovereignty of God, and often the very existence of God has been reduced to a myth in most of the homes of this country, bringing world leaders to refer to Canada as atheistic. Canada has "no fear of God before their eyes". Society that accepts its roots as from animal origin will degenerate to the morality of animals, (even to the extreme of destroying their own young), society that sees its end in this physical existence will make the pleasures of this life their chief end, (giving no thought to eternity). When God is removed from view, accountability to God is also lost to sight.

The great wonder is that to such a God-forgetting society, the Lord still extends His invitation to turn again to Him. To each individual, God tenderly declares "the wages of sin [is] death; but the gift of God [is] eternal life through Jesus Christ our Lord." (Romans 6:23). His love for this world is so intense that "God demonstrated his love toward us, in that, while we were yet sinners, Christ died for us." (Romans 5:8).

God's truth will not fail, He alone has determined the conditions of entering into His presence, Jesus set the matter straight when he said "I am the way, the truth, and the life: no man cometh unto the Father, but by me." (John 14:6). Peter understood the implications of abandoning God. "Then said Jesus unto the twelve, Will ye also go away? Then Simon Peter answered him, Lord, to whom shall we go? thou hast the words of eternal life. And we believe and are sure that thou art that Christ, the Son of the living God. (John 6:67-69).

Countries such as Russia, and to some extent Brazil, who have pursued a path of denying God, are now seeking Bible truth with a passion. Where once scriptures were outlawed, now they are being read and studied in public schools, libraries and even government agencies. Likewise, if our nation is to recover at all from its moral and ethical degeneration, there will have to be a return to God by a revitalizing of Bible teaching. Otherwise, Solomon's prophetic statement will come true. "Where [there is] no vision (revelation of God), the people perish (cast off restraint): but he that keepeth the law, happy [is] he" (Proverbs 29:18).

Personal Notes

Ecclesiastes 3:1-13

To everything there is a season, A time for every purpose under heaven: A time to be born, And a time to die; A time to plant, And a time to pluck what is planted; A time to kill, And a time to heal; A time to break down, And a time to build up; A time to weep, And a time to laugh; A time to mourn, And a time to dance; A time to cast away stones, And a time to gather stones; A time to embrace, And a time to refrain from embracing; A time to gain, And a time to lose; A time to keep, And a time to throw away; A time to tear, And a time to sew; A time to keep silence, And a time to speak; A time to love, And a time to hate; A time of war, And a time of peace. What profit has the worker from that in which he labours? I have seen the God–given task with which the sons of men are to be occupied.

He has made everything beautiful in its time. Also He has put eternity in their hearts, except that no one can find out the work that God does from beginning to end. I know that nothing is better for them than to rejoice, and to do good in their lives, and also that every man should eat and drink and enjoy the good of all his labour—it is the gift of God."

The Medicine of Laughter

While exercising pastoral duties some time ago during a morning worship service, I had just finished sharing announcements when, returning to my seat on the platform, I somehow misjudged my location and caught only part of the chair as I sat down. The result was a frantic attempt to regain balance by the waving of arms as my foot shot straight up into the air. After what seemed like an eternity, I resolved to give up the balance attempt and resigned to fall on the floor. About the only thing a pastor can do after such a grand display of poise is to take a bow and hope the laughter dies down before the sermon begins. This I did, though somewhat red of face! The unique (and hopefully redeeming) aspect of this entire experience was the unified sound of laughter. For a brief moment I experienced that feeling of euphoria mentioned often by the master of comedy, Red Skelton, in bringing people to the point of merriment and laughter by good, clean fun.

Solomon spoke of the medicinal effect of laughter: "A merry heart doeth good [like] a medicine:" (Proverbs 17:22), "he that is of a merry heart [hath] a continual feast." (Proverbs 15:15). In referring to all that characterizes life, the Bible states that "there is a time to weep and a time to laugh, a time to mourn and a time to dance" (Ecclesiastes 3:4). Clearly, laughter plays a meaningful part in man's emotional framework as designed by God.

The "best of times" that our memories draw us back to include much laughter. People search for moments when the heart can be merry and rejoice aloud. Unfortunately, our society seems to pursue the merry heart through light-headedness rather than light-heartedness. Instead of finding a heart made light by the removal of burdens through a meaningful relationship to God, many seek to make the head light through substance abuse. God describes the futility of such a pursuit. "There is a way which seemeth right unto a man, but the end thereof [are] the ways of death. Even in laughter the heart is sorrowful; and the end of that mirth [is] heaviness." (Proverbs 14:12-13).

God intended something better for man. A truly merry heart can be found as men and women learn to cast their care upon the Lord, because He cares deeply for us. (1 Peter 5:7) To all who acknowledge personal captivity to sin and come to Christ for forgiveness and release (see Romans chapter 8), there is a lifting of burden and rejoicing of heart made available in every circumstance, not unlike that of Israel: "When the LORD turned again the captivity of Zion, we were like them that dream. Then was our mouth filled with laughter, and our tongue with singing: then said they among the heathen, The LORD hath done great things for them." (Psalms 126:1-2).

As I returned to the pulpit on that eventful Sunday, seeking to lead the congregation into meaningful worship, a young lad near the front cried out "There's that funny guy, Mom!" The laughter returned, but that's fine. Let the people of God be merry with laughter; this too, is good medicine and fulfils the purposes of God.

Personal Notes

Romans 10:6-15

But the righteousness of faith speaks in this way, "Do not say in your heart, 'Who will ascend into heaven?'"(that is, to bring Christ down from above) or, "'Who will descend into the abyss?'"(that is, to bring Christ up from the dead). But what does it say? "The word is near you, in your mouth and in your heart" (that is, the word of faith which we preach): that if you confess with your mouth the Lord Jesus and believe in your heart that God has raised Him from the dead, you will be saved. For with the heart one believes unto righteousness, and with the mouth confession is made unto salvation. For the Scripture says, "Whoever believes on Him will not be put to shame." For there is no distinction between Jew and Greek, for the same Lord over all is rich to all who call upon Him. For "whoever calls on the name of the LORD shall be saved." How then shall they call on Him in whom they have not believed? And how shall they believe in Him of whom they have not heard? And how shall they hear without a preacher? And how shall they preach unless they are sent? As it is written: "How beautiful are the feet of those who preach the gospel of peace, Who bring glad tidings of good things!"

The Unfamiliar Waters of Witnessing

Over 1,000 British soldiers died at Bunker Hill because Admiral Graves refused to send a ship up the Mystic River to protect the infantry. He feared losing his ship and reputation in unfamiliar waters. We brand this action as cowardly and irresponsible, yet a far greater tragedy occurs daily as countless numbers of people, known well by born-again believers, pass into eternity without knowledge of Christ. The reason: many Christians are afraid to travel the unfamiliar waters of witnessing.

Paul reminds believers that "God did not give us the Spirit of cowardice, but of power, and of love, and of a sound mind." Those who are submissive to the Spirit's control find power to overcome the fear of speaking to people about Christ. Christians should be moved by God's love to see the unsaved as sheep without a shepherd, lost and astray. They should be ever mindful of the imminent danger of death and the great gap between sinful man and Holy God which results in separation forever from God. "For Thou [art] not a God that hath pleasure in wickedness: neither shall evil dwell with thee." (Psalms 5:4). Believers need to focus on God's love in bridging the gap between imperfect man and His Holy character which cost Him dearly. "For Christ also hath once suffered for sins, the just for the unjust, that he might bring us to God" (1 Peter 3:18).

In being reminded of that sacrificial love of God, a Christian is called to share the gospel. This means explaining that giving God our heart involves an acknowledgement of our inability to compensate for our own wrongs and an acceptance of Christ's sacrificial death as full payment for sin (1 John 2:2), as well as a confidence in Christ's resurrection as victory over sin and eternal death (Romans 6).

The responsibility of witnessing is not one of talking alone. The credibility of Christianity comes from the power of God to transform a life. It is the Lord's intention to let the unbelieving world evidence the reality of salvation through the genuine changing of character and values of individual believers, resulting in obvious hope. This calls for a continued giving of the heart to God: "But sanctify the Lord God in your hearts: and [be] ready always to [give] an answer to every man that asketh you a reason of the hope that is in you with meekness and fear:" (1 Peter 3:15)

No one suspected such tragedy on that June 17, 1775. When the smoke cleared the officers could only say "If only we had known." Christian friend, you do know the end for those who never accept Christ. Won't you tell someone today that "God so loved the world, He gave His only begotten Son, that whosoever believeth in Him should not perish but have everlasting live" (John 3:16)?

Personal Notes

Ruth 1:8-18

And Naomi said to her two daughters–in–law, "Go, return each to her mother's house. The LORD deal kindly with you, as you have dealt with the dead and with me. "The LORD grant that you may find rest, each in the house of her husband." Then she kissed them, and they lifted up their voices and wept. And they said to her, "Surely we will return with you to your people." But Naomi said, "Turn back, my daughters; why will you go with me? Are there still sons in my womb, that they may be your husbands? "Turn back, my daughters, go—for I am too old to have a husband. If I should say I have hope, if I should have a husband tonight and should also bear sons, "would you wait for them till they were grown? Would you restrain yourselves from having husbands? No, my daughters; for it grieves me very much for your sakes that the hand of the LORD has gone out against me!" Then they lifted up their voices and wept again; and Orpah kissed her mother–in–law, but Ruth clung to her. And she said, "Look, your sister–in–law has gone back to her people and to her gods; return after your sister–in–law." But Ruth said: "Entreat me not to leave you, Or to turn back from following after you; For wherever you go, I will go; And wherever you lodge, I will lodge; Your people shall be my people, And your God, my God. Where you die, I will die, And there will I be buried. The LORD do so to me, and more also, If anything but death parts you and me." When she saw that she was determined to go with her, she stopped speaking to her.

History's Repetition

It would seem obvious to any history buff that "history repeats itself". This certainly is the evident pattern of Israel's history. In particular, the book of Judges identifies the history of Israel as a cycle of sin, suffering, and supplication to God which brought eventual salvation. This cycle however followed a morally downward spiral until all that could be said was that "In those days Israel had no king; everyone did as he saw fit." (Judges 17:6 NIV). That seems like a reasonable description of our society as well.

How encouraging it is to find the story of Ruth following the description of the Judges. After a dismal record of failure and spiritual collapse, we are given a story of love, devotion and strength. In the midst of family hardship and loss, Ruth made a bold commitment. "Don't urge me to leave you or to turn back from you. Where you go I will go, and where you stay I will stay. Your people will be my people and your God my God." (Ruth 1:16 NIV). Although Ruth had lost her husband, her brother-in-law and her father-in-law, she refused to return to the ways of her own people, but chose to stay with her mother-in-law, Naomi, and cling to the Lord. Ruth's abandonment of self-interest for love and care toward Naomi brought an unexpected blessing. She learned in returning to Bethlehem that Naomi's God was more than a stone statue or national symbol, He was the living and true God.

Ruth's return with Naomi was met with a blessing that became fully realized in her life: "May the LORD repay you for what you have done. May you be richly rewarded by the LORD, the God of Israel, under whose wings you have come to take refuge." (Ruth 2:12 NIV). Naomi's God became to Ruth the Lord of repayment, and the Lord of reward and the Lord of refuge, just as He has promised to be to all who would put their trust in Him. In this, history has also repeated itself. David found the Lord to be so, "God is our refuge and strength, an ever-present help in trouble." (Psalms 46:1 NIV), as did Paul: "I know what it is to be in need, and I know what it is to have plenty. I have learned the secret of being content in any and every situation, whether well fed or hungry, whether living in plenty or in want. I can do everything through him who gives me strength. (Philippians 4:12-13 NIV), as have many more (see Hebrews 11). Countless numbers of people, while the world around them does what it pleases, have sought the Lord and found great blessing.

History can be repeated as a downward spiral away from God as people do what they see fit, or as a rewarding discovery of the living and true God who is "repayer", "rewarder" and "refuge" because He is THE REDEEMER. In which way is history being repeated in your life?

Personal Notes

Romans 5:8-18

But God demonstrates His own love toward us, in that while we were still sinners, Christ died for us. Much more then, having now been justified by His blood, we shall be saved from wrath through Him. For if when we were enemies we were reconciled to God through the death of His Son, much more, having been reconciled, we shall be saved by His life. And not only that, but we also rejoice in God through our Lord Jesus Christ, through whom we have now received the reconciliation. Therefore, just as through one man sin entered the world, and death through sin, and thus death spread to all men, because all sinned— (For until the law sin was in the world, but sin is not imputed when there is no law. Nevertheless death reigned from Adam to Moses, even over those who had not sinned according to the likeness of the transgression of Adam, who is a type of Him who was to come. But the free gift is not like the offense. For if by the one man's offense many died, much more the grace of God and the gift by the grace of the one Man, Jesus Christ, abounded to many. And the gift is not like that which came through the one who sinned. For the judgment which came from one offense resulted in condemnation, but the free gift which came from many offenses resulted in justification. For if by the one man's offense death reigned through the one, much more those who receive abundance of grace and of the gift of righteousness will reign in life through the One, Jesus Christ.) Therefore, as through one man's offense judgment came to all men, resulting in condemnation, even so through one Man's righteous act the free gift came to all men, resulting in justification of life.

The Gift of Salvation

The popular seasonal song "Santa Claus is coming to Town" suggests that children must be sure to be good or Santa will not leave a gift. Although I would not want to take anything away from the important message of good behaviour, to suggest that the receiving of gifts is conditional upon "being good" contradicts the intent of what a true gift is. It has been said that every gift, though it be small, is in reality great if given with affection. A true gift is given out of the unconditional love of the giver. Any condition placed upon a gift turns it into an earned reward or payment and robs both the giver and receiver of an expression of love.

The same is true of God's gift of salvation: "For it is by grace you have been saved, through faith--and this not from yourselves, it is the gift of God-- not by works, so that no-one can boast." (Ephesians 2 NIV). Salvation is by grace; therefore, it is undeserved and salvation is a gift; therefore, it is unearned.

The Bible indicates at least two reasons why this salvation is a true gift. The first reason is clear: no person can earn the right to stand before our Holy God because no person is perfect and God's character demands perfection. Scripture states, "There is not a righteous man on earth who does what is right and never sins" (Ecclesiastes 7:20 NIV).

The Bible points out that man's best efforts to win God's favour are clouded with wrong motives and selfish desire, the resultant effort is assessed by God. "All of us have become like one who is unclean, and all our righteous acts are like filthy rags; we all shrivel up like a leaf, and like the wind our sins sweep us away." (Isaiah 64:6 NIV).

As much as mankind may think of itself as worthy of merit, the fact remains that the capacity to measure up to God's standard of perfection is not within man "for all have sinned and fall short of the glory of God" (Romans 3:23 NIV). That's what makes the second reason for salvation as a true gift so precious. Salvation was secured and is offered as an expression of the unconditional love of God. "But God demonstrates his own love for us in this: While we were still sinners, Christ died for us" (Romans 5:8 NIV).

Salvation is found not in the earning power of man's behaviour, but as the unconditional nature of God's love. "For the wages of sin is death, but the gift of God is eternal life in Christ Jesus our Lord" (Romans 6:23 NIV). Like a gift received with appreciation at Christmas, so each person must accept God's true gift. "Yet to all who received him, to those who believed in his name, he gave the right to become children of God" (John 1:12 NIV).

Personal Notes

Matthew 7:24-27

"Therefore whoever hears these sayings of Mine, and does them, I will liken him to a wise man who built his house on the rock: "and the rain descended, the floods came, and the winds blew and beat on that house; and it did not fall, for it was founded on the rock. "But everyone who hears these sayings of Mine, and does not do them, will be like a foolish man who built his house on the sand: "and the rain descended, the floods came, and the winds blew and beat on that house; and it fell. And great was its fall."

Destructive Passions

Although the old children's story about the three little pigs and the big bad wolf probably had political innuendoes that have long since ceased to be appreciated, the one truth about the story is the importance of making a home out of the right stuff. Considering that half the couples in North America being married today end in separation or divorce, it would seem that homes are being built with the wrong materials! I speak of the material upon which human relationships are being built.

The apostle John had some insight regarding good and bad building material. "For all that [is] in the world, the lust of the flesh, and the lust of the eyes, and the pride of life, is not of the Father, but is of the world. And the world passes away, and the lust thereof: but he that does the will of God abides for ever" (1 John 2).

There are three passions here mentioned by John that pass quickly away, and yet many couples build their entire relationship upon them. There are those that seek only physical gratification and build relationships entirely upon "what feels good", without any moral conscience. Others, although perhaps morally restrained, seek a relationship founded upon pleasures that gratify the sight (and therefore the mind) - a "look cool" value system that focuses on being invited to the "right" places and doing the "right" things. Still others build relationships on what's best for a career and what is most advantageous financially - that old "I loved the girl next door, but I married the banker's daughter" approach.

John states that these passions soon pass, they have no enduring qualities. The slightest huff or puff and these relationships disintegrate. Only those who build relationships according to God's plan will endure. That plan begins with a relationship to God through new life in His Son, and grows into a capacity to love others as God loves us. "This is love: not that we loved God, but that he loved us and sent his Son as an atoning sacrifice for our sins. Dear friends, since God so loved us, we also ought to love one another." (1 John 4 NIV) It is this love that God calls man to build relationships upon.

Paul speaks of the enduring quality and special characteristics of God's number one building material. "Love is patient, love is kind. It does not envy, it does not boast, it is not proud. It is not rude, it is not self-seeking, it is not easily angered, it keeps no record of wrongs. Love does not delight in evil but rejoices with the truth. It always protects, always trusts, always hopes, always perseveres. Love never fails." (1 Corinthians 13 NIV). This is the building "stuff" that lasts a life time, out of this a relationship flourishes.

No matter how happily a home begins, eventually the big bad wolf comes a huffing and a puffing! Whether your home fades or flourishes will depend upon the building material!

Personal Notes

Psalm 68:1-6

May God arise, may his enemies be scattered; may his foes flee before him. As smoke is blown away by the wind, may you blow them away; as wax melts before the fire, may the wicked perish before God. But may the righteous be glad and rejoice before God; may they be happy and joyful. Sing to God, sing praise to his name, extol him who rides on the clouds— his name is the LORD—and rejoice before him. A father to the fatherless, a defender of widows, is God in his holy dwelling. God sets the lonely in families, he leads forth the prisoners with singing; but the rebellious live in a sun-scorched land.

Support for The Lonely

There is a monster in our home that has followed us everywhere we have moved! It attacks at the most inopportune time; just as I get ready for a special occasion, or am in a rush to be on my way for an important appointment, there it strikes - the sock monster - tearing apart my best pairs of socks and leaving me holding two unmatched, sad pieces of material with which to cover my feet! Why this monster always attacks the best pairs of sock I do not know, but this I do know; my drawer is full of perfectly good, hardly used single socks.

Now I can laugh at the sock monster, (mostly because my pant legs are long enough to cover the mismatches), but that drawer of mine reminds me of all the fine people I know who have been the victim of the real "pair" splitter. Such folks find themselves, after what promised to be a long and happy marriage, single with children, and desperately lonely. For them my heart aches, and my prayers ascend.

In spite of the great turmoil that descends upon such folks (particularly women, but not always) there is consolation in the promises of God. Because of the harsh life of the Israelite men in Old Testament times, many women found themselves widowed or abandoned with children. To these lonely and troubled women God gave this special promise: "A father to the fatherless, a defender of widows, is God in his holy dwelling. God sets the lonely in families," (Psalms 68 NIV).

The Lord has a special place in His own heart for the widows (or the abandoned) and their children. He promises to care for the children as a father, to defend the women as a husband, and to see that they are embraced by other families who will provide help and support. So important is this in the mind of the Lord that He defines true religion by it. "Religion that God our Father accepts as pure and faultless is this: to look after orphans and widows in their distress and to keep oneself from being polluted by the world." (James 1:27 NIV)

To the once "perfect pair" who now find themselves torn apart and very lonely, take heart, there is special care from God. He only asks that you come to Him through His Son, who died on the cross to bear our guilt of sin and offer forgiveness through faith. His offer stands: "since we have a great high priest who has gone through the heavens, Jesus the Son of God, let us hold firmly to the faith we profess... Let us then approach the throne of grace with confidence, so that we may receive mercy and find grace to help us in our time of need." (Hebrews 4 NIV). To all who seek His care and trust in His provision, He makes this additional promise: "Never will I leave you; never will I forsake you." (Hebrews 13:5 NIV). Turn to Him today!

Personal Notes

1 Corinthians 10:23-33

All things are lawful for me, but not all things are helpful; all things are lawful for me, but not all things edify. Let no one seek his own, but each one the other's well-being. Eat whatever is sold in the meat market, asking no questions for conscience' sake; for "the earth is the LORD'S, and all its fullness." If any of those who do not believe invites you to dinner, and you desire to go, eat whatever is set before you, asking no question for conscience' sake. But if anyone says to you, "This was offered to idols," do not eat it for the sake of the one who told you, and for conscience' sake; for "the earth is the LORD'S, and all its fullness." "Conscience," I say, not your own, but that of the other. For why is my liberty judged by another man's conscience? But if I partake with thanks, why am I evil spoken of for the food over which I give thanks? Therefore, whether you eat or drink, or whatever you do, do all to the glory of God. Give no offense, either to the Jews or to the Greeks or to the church of God, just as I also please all men in all things, not seeking my own profit, but the profit of many, that they may be saved.

See-it Love

Henry Ford II once stated: "No society of nations, no people within a nation, no family can benefit through mutual aid unless good will exceeds ill will; unless the spirit of cooperation surpasses antagonism; unless we all see and act as though the other man's welfare determines our own welfare." Christ said the same thing in less words: "Love your neighbour as yourself."

Without a doubt, our greatest influence on those around us comes through a heart of love, not the emotional nor the erotic love that so many are caught up in today, but through the self-sacrificing love that Jesus epitomized as the Son of God who died as substitute for man. "But God commendeth his love toward us, in that, while we were yet sinners, Christ died for us" (Romans 5:8).

Paul simplified the expression of that love to believers in a very practical way. "Nobody should seek his own good, but the good of others" (1 Corinthians 10:24 NIV). Imagine the transformation of families, businesses, governments and societies if even the Christians within our land truly lived this principle!

Stephen Olford in *The Grace of Giving* relates the following true story. During the American Revolution, a pastor named Peter

Miller walked seventy miles to plead the life of Michael Wittman, a man accused of treason, and a man who had formerly used all his power to oppose the ministry of Miller. George Washington stated that he could not pardon Miller's friend, to which Miller responded: "My friend! He is my bitterest enemy." Upon hearing this, Washington replied: "What? You've walked seventy miles to save the life of your enemy? That puts the matter in a different light. I grant the pardon." Miller rescued Wittman from the jaws of judgement and death and brought home a man no longer his enemy, but his friend.

It is this very thing that Christ has done for each person who, with repentant heart, believes that Jesus died to bear their sin and rose to offer life. "But God commendeth his love toward us, in that, while we were yet sinners, Christ died for us" (Romans 5:8). It is this very thing that God calls each believer to practice in their own life. Paul's challenge to the church at Philippi is God's challenge to each Christian today. "If you have any encouragement from being united with Christ, if any comfort from his love, if any fellowship with the Spirit, if any tenderness and compassion, then make my joy complete... Do nothing out of selfish ambition or vain conceit, but in humility consider others better than yourselves. Each of you should look not only to your own interests, but also to the interests of others" (Philippians 2 NIV).

In Jesus, "God so loved the world",
He died to set man free.
Now, help me show to all that path;
Lord, love the world through me.

Christian friend, look for practical way at home, at work in the community to "love your neighbour as yourself!"

Personal Notes

Made in the USA
Charleston, SC
25 June 2016